MANAGING PEOPLE IN THE WORKPLACE

About the Authors

Linda Reidy BA (Psy), DBA, MSc, lectures in Human Resource Management and Behavioural Science at Athlone Institute of Technology and is the author of *Make that Grade – Human Resource Management*, Gill and Macmillan, 2003.

Marian O'Sullivan MA (HRM), MSc, MCIPD, is a Senior Lecturer in HRM at Coventry University. She spent many years working within the HR and training functions of a number of organisations, in both Ireland and the UK.

MANAGING PEOPLE IN THE WORKPLACE

Linda Reidy

and

Marian O'Sullivan

BLACKHALL
Publishing

This book was typeset by Gough Typesetting Services for

Blackhall Publishing
27 Carysfort Avenue
Blackrock
Co. Dublin
Ireland

e-mail: info@blackhallpublishing.com
www.blackhallpublishing.com

© Linda Reidy and Marian O'Sullivan, 2004

ISBN: 1 842180 69 X

A catalogue record for this book is available from the British Library.

Printed in Ireland by
ColourBooks Ltd

PREFACE

This book is aimed at owners and managers of small and medium-sized businesses based in Ireland who do not have a dedicated human resources function. It provides basic practical guidance and advice on the main aspects of managing people in the workplace. Some of the things this book will help you to do are write a job description, conduct an interview, resolve industrial disputes and improve your knowledge of Irish employment legislation.

The Contents section is structured to allow you to identify the information you are looking for quickly. You can read each chapter on its own, without having to read the whole book. Each chapter provides links to other chapters to enable you to supplement the information you are interested in. A detailed index is included at the back to help you to find information on specific issues.

Sample documentation is included and can be adapted to suit your organisation.

ACKNOWLEDGEMENTS

The authors wish to express their gratitude to those who provided valuable feedback and suggestions at all stages of this project.

CONTENTS

Appendices

Part I

INTRODUCTION

Chapter 1

INTRODUCTION TO
HUMAN RESOURCE MANAGEMENT

> "Human resource management (HRM) involves all management decisions and practices that directly affect or influence the people, or human resources, who work for the organization."
>
> (Fisher, Schoenfeldt and Shaw, 1999: 7)

This chapter will help you to:

- understand what HRM is

- distinguish between personnel management and HRM

- understand the factors that influence the style of management used by organisations

- introduce a HRM style of management in your organisation.

WHAT IS HRM?

During the 1980s and 1990s, a time of worldwide recession, many business leaders recognised that their employees were a key to competitive advantage. This view of the employee as a valuable resource led to the emergence of a new style of management, which became known as human resource management (HRM).

This development in management style has certainly been influenced by the fact that both workers and the organisations that employ them have changed considerably over the last 20 years. The standard of education has increased and employees expect better working conditions and better treatment from employers. Furthermore, today's workers are more likely to take an interest in the performance of their organisation and often want to be involved in the decision making that directly affects them.

Organisations have changed, too. Due to technological developments, change occurs more quickly now and an organisation has to be able to adapt to the changing environment in order to survive. An organisation's ability to adapt to change relies heavily on its employees.

Differences between Personnel Management and HRM

In theory, HRM is not a synonym for personnel management. Instead, it should be viewed as another perspective on managing people. In reality, the "personnel" and "HRM" titles do not always reflect the style of management dominant in an organisation. In other words, just because an organisation has a personnel manager, it does not necessarily follow that the traditional style of management is used. Similarly, just because an organisation employs a HR manager, it does not mean that HR policies and strategies are supported in the organisation.

Characteristics of the "Personnel" Style of Management

• People management tends not to be linked to the business plan.

• There is a tendency to deal with situations as they occur rather than anticipating problems or situations before they happen.

• This style is based on the idea that managers and employees have conflicting interests within the workplace.

• It is characterised by low levels of trust between managers and employees.

• Unionisation is common.

• There is little flexibility in how work is done.

• Power and decision making lie with few individuals.

Characteristics of the HR Style of Management

• All HR activities support the business plan.

• There is a tendency to try to anticipate problems and deal with them before they arise.

• This style is based on the idea that managers and employees have similar goals within the workplace.

• It is characterised by high levels of trust between managers and employees.

• Employee commitment to the organisation is encouraged.

• Unionisation is reduced.

- There is flexibility in how work is done.

- Power and decision making are shared.

FACTORS THAT INFLUENCE MANAGEMENT STYLE

Company Size

Company size can affect how people are managed. For example, relations between employees and management in smaller companies tend to be less formal and there is less likely to be union representation, so it can be easier for them to adopt some of the ideas and principles of HRM. Large organisations, however, have to apply the same policies and strategies to their employees across the board. Union representation, common in larger organisations, underlines the notion that workers and management have different agendas. Thus, principles of HRM can be difficult to integrate into a larger organisation.

Culture

Organisational culture refers to the accepted way of doing things within a place of work. If the culture traditionally encouraged compliance with procedures and discouraged initiative, it would be difficult to make a sudden change to this culture of commitment and participation. An organisation's culture develops gradually over time and can be hard to change quickly. For this reason, new organisations can more easily adapt to the characteristics of the HRM style than older organisations.

Technology

The type of technology used affects how people are managed. Guest (1987) suggests, for example, that assembly line job design does not fit in well with the HRM style of management, as it does not give either workers or managers much flexibility in their roles.

Labour Market

If there are plenty of qualified people available for work, the organisation is under less pressure to offer more attractive salaries or to invest in training and development. This was the situation for many Irish companies in the late 1980s and early 1990s during a period of high unemployment. When suitably qualified people are scarce, they become more valuable to the organisation and are treated accordingly.

Product Market

The organisation's product market can influence the approach to people management. If the company's products have a high market share, for example, then the organisation is in a better position to be more generous to employees in terms of pay or training. However, if there are difficulties in the product market, management has to focus on the task rather than the employees.

Employment Legislation

Laws on health and safety, dismissal, maternity and equality are examples of the legal influences on managing employees in areas such as recruitment, selection and termination of employment. Employers have certain legal obligations to their employees and this has some bearing on management style.

INTRODUCING A HR STYLE OF MANAGEMENT

According to Guest (1987), organisations will be more successful if they try to achieve four key HRM goals:

1. integrate people management style with overall business strategy
2. encourage employee commitment to the organisation
3. aim for flexibility in both the job content and organisation structure
4. aim for high standards of quality in the work that is carried out, the people that are employed and the treatment of employees by management.

You can achieve these four goals by:

- giving careful consideration to job design
- choosing the right people for the job
- training and developing your staff
- managing employee performance
- giving careful consideration to the reward system
- communicating with employees
- managing change effectively.

These elements of managing employees are covered in the following chapters.

If all four goals are achieved, your organisation can expect to improve cost-effectiveness, performance and problem solving, and lower staff turnover and absenteeism. Appropriate leadership, strategic vision and culture are necessary for a HRM style of management to be effective.

Chapter 2

Keeping Personnel Records: Essential Documentation

Personnel records are "the set of documents accumulated for each employee covering all aspects of their employment."

(Heery and Noon, 2001: 268)

This chapter will help you to:

- understand the purpose of keeping personnel records
- comply with data protection legislation
- identify and compile essential personnel information
- link personnel information to other HR practices.

The Purpose of Personnel Records

Record keeping is an important part of running a business, as access to accurate and timely information is an integral part of decision making and planning within organisations. By examining employee records, employers can identify if they are likely to have sufficient numbers of appropriately qualified and experienced employees to achieve their business objectives.

According to Graham and Bennett (1998: 173), personnel records provide the following:

- a store of up-to-date and accurate information about the company's employees
- a guide to the action to be taken regarding an employee, particularly by comparing the worker with other employees
- a guide when recruiting a new employee, for example by showing the rates of pay received by comparable employees
- a historical record of previous action taken regarding employees
- the raw materials for statistics which check and guide personnel policies

• the means to comply with certain statutory requirements.

DATA PROTECTION LEGISLATION

Obtaining and processing personal data, whether manually or by computer, is subject to the Data Protection (Amendment) Act, 2003. Individuals have increased rights over any personal information held by organisations and organisations have many additional obligations to those on whom they hold information. The key points to be aware of include the following:

• The Data Protection (Amendment) Act, 2003 now extends to both manual and computerised records. The term "manual data" "means information kept as part of a 'relevant filing system', or kept with the intention that it should form part of such a system".

• Employers may only process data relating to their employees if they comply with the Data Protection Principles, which provide that the data must have been obtained and processed fairly.

• It is important that employers obtain consent from individuals to hold and process personal data.

• Employees have the right to be informed of any data held on them.

• Employees can also inspect any data on them held by employers and can object to how it is being processed. Where data is found to be incorrect, employees can insist on its rectification, erasure or blockage.

• Failure to comply with The Data Protection (Amendment) Act, 2003 may result in the Data Protection Commissioner taking legal action and the organisation paying heavy fines.

It is recommended that organisations seek professional advice on their record-keeping activities to ensure legislative compliance. Further information on the Data Protection (Amendment) Act, 2003 can be obtained from the Data Protection Commissioner's website www.dataprivacy.ie.

CONTENTS OF PERSONNEL RECORDS

The initial contents of an employee's personnel record will comprise the following:

• employee's curriculum vitae or application form

- copy of contract of employment
- copy of employee's acceptance of position.

It is a good idea to attach a copy of the advertisement, the job description and person specification for future reference.
    As time goes on, other documentation can be added to the file, for example:

- performance appraisals
- details of training courses undertaken
- certificates of sickness
- grievance and disciplinary records.

Organisations can hold information on their employees either on individual record cards or on a computerised system. It is important that this information is organised in such a way that specific information such as length of service, grade or pay rate can be accessed quickly. Employee information can be organised into two types: personal and organisational.

Personal

- Employee name, address, telephone number and e-mail
- Date of birth
- Details of next of kin
- Date joined organisation
- Qualifications
- Previous employment

Organisational

- Employment history in organisation (department/position/dates)
- Salary details
- Holiday entitlement
- Training received
- Skills and competencies
- Performance appraisal information

- Absences
- Retirement date
- Pension details
- Disciplinary warnings
- Date of leaving organisation
- Reason for leaving organisation
- Would organisation re-employ?

Some organisations are now availing of computerised personnel information systems (CPIS), which have several advantages such as:

- being able to handle vast quantities of data quickly
- providing faster access to employee data
- incorporating payroll management.

However, there are a number of issues that need to be addressed before acquiring and using CPIS. Computerised personnel information systems are expensive and consequently it is important that the system you choose meet the needs of the organisation. Users of the system must be fully trained to ensure that the organisation is making best use of the system and is complying with data protection legislation. The data generated from the system is only as good as the information that is input; accurate and up-to-date data is therefore essential.

LINKING PERSONNEL RECORDS TO OTHER HR ACTIVITIES

Personnel information provides the foundation for all other HR activities such as:

- human resource planning
- recruitment and selection
- staff development
- reward management
- performance appraisal
- health and safety
- termination of employment.

The following chapters in this book will illustrate how this information is used to undertake these HR activities.

CONTACT

Data Protection Commissioner
Block 6
Irish Life Centre
Lower Abbey Street
Dublin 1
Tel: (01) 8748544
e-mail: www.dataprivacy.ie

Part II

Employing Staff

Chapter 3

HUMAN RESOURCE PLANNING: PLANNING FOR THE FUTURE

"Human resource planning (HRP) is the process of analysing an organisation's need for employees and evaluating how this can be met from the internal and external labour markets."

(Heery and Noon, 2001: 164)

This chapter will help you to:

- understand the importance of human resource planning
- develop a human resource plan
- examine current human resources
- draw up a job description and person specification
- forecast demand and supply of labour.

THE IMPORTANCE OF HUMAN RESOURCE PLANNING

Your organisation needs to be prepared as far as possible to deal with future staff and skill requirements so that you can achieve your strategic objectives. If you want to increase your market share, increase production or develop new products, you will need to have the right number of employees with the appropriate skills and qualifications when they are required. Poor human resource planning can be costly if work is lost due to staff shortages, or if your organisation is overstaffed. The information acquired through planning will help you to:

- avoid staff shortages
- anticipate a surplus of employees
- identify skill shortages
- specify training needs
- select suitable employees

- prepare the organisation for change
- meet both employee and organisational expectations within the workplace.

THE HR PLANNING PROCESS

This section describes the four stages in the HR planning process:

1. analyse current situation
2. forecast demand and supply of labour
3. devise plans
4. implement and review.

Figure 3.1: Stages of the HR Planning Process

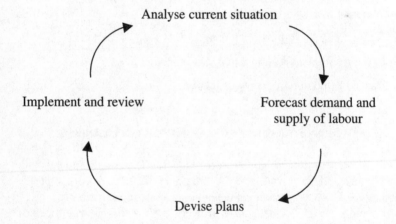

Analyse current situation

Implement and review

Forecast demand and supply of labour

Devise plans

Analyse Current Situation

Before you plan for your future staffing and skill requirements, you need to examine the current situation within your organisation and be familiar with developments outside the organisation that may affect your business.

The Internal Environment

To keep track of what is going on inside the organisation you will need to:

- review your employee profile
- carry out a job analysis.

Employee profile   Assessing current human resources begins by reviewing the profile of the organisation's employees. This is sometimes called "stocktaking". Just as the retailer keeps a record of every item in stock in the shop at a particular time, it is important to maintain a profile of every employee within the organisation. This information is gathered from personnel records (see Chapter 2), performance appraisals (Chapter 7) and forms completed by employees specifically for this purpose.

An employee database is a valuable tool for assessing the skills that are currently available in the organisation. Managers may not always be aware that their employees possess skills other than those necessary to carry out the jobs they were employed to do. The information gathered is also useful for making decisions with regard to the selection of individuals for training, promotion and transfer as well as the development of recruitment plans.

Job analysis   Job analysis is a systematic examination of jobs within an organisation. It is carried out to identify the human behaviour necessary for adequate job performance. You can gather information for the job analysis in a number of ways. These include:

- interviewing jobholders to obtain details of how jobs are completed
- observing how employees carry out their work
- having workers complete questionnaires designed for the purpose of job analysis
- asking employees to keep job diaries
- having discussions with managers and supervisors.

The job analysis is divided into three parts and involves describing the job in detail, specifying the kind of person required to do it and outlining the terms and conditions of the job.

The components of a job analysis are:

- job description
- person specification or competency framework
- terms and conditions of employment.

Job description   The job description forms the basis for the contract of employment. The main elements are:

- job title
- department/function
- who the employee reports to
- who reports to the employee (if applicable)
- who the employee liaises or works with
- overall purpose of the job
- main tasks and responsibilities.

Figure 3.2: Sample Job Description

Job Title	Senior Administrator
Dept/function	General Insurance
Reports to	Branch Manager
Liaises with	Clients, insurance companies, IT help desks, employees and management

Overall purpose of job

The jobholder will manage all enquiries, correspondence and the IT system to ensure that an efficient administrative service is provided to all clients and management.

Main tasks and responsibilities

The Senior Administrator will:

- manage all client claims and account enquiries in respect of new and existing business, received by telephone, e-mail or in person
- prepare and issue all appropriate quotations, policies, where appropriate, and general correspondence in respect of new and existing business, claims and accounts
- utilise technology to undertake regular research on insurance developments and marketing initiatives for management
- back up all computerised information on a daily basis
- ensure that all computer systems are operating correctly
- provide IT training to all new staff
- carry out other duties as directed by the Branch Manager.

The job description and flexibility   Employers are sometimes wary of the inflexibility that results from a clearly defined job description. Small organisations in particular rely on employees adopting a flexible approach to their job. When a job description specifies the responsibilities attached to a particular job, the employee may refuse to do any work that is not clearly spelled out. Armstrong (1999: 300) suggests a way to overcome this potential inflexibility in job descriptions. He recommends that flexibility should be built into the job description by "concentrating on results rather than spelling out what has to be done". By emphasising the outcome of the job rather than detailing the tasks that lead to that outcome, you can increase the flexibility of the job description and ensure that employees cannot refuse to do work on the basis that it is not in their job description.

Person specification   The person specification outlines the skills and experience necessary to carry out the tasks and responsibilities of the job. It provides details of the type of person the organisation wishes to employ. The person specification should match the job description and include details of the following:

• qualifications

• knowledge

• specific skills and aptitudes

Figure 3.3: Sample of Person Specification

Job Title	Senior Administrator	
Department	General Insurance	
	Essential	*Desirable*
Qualifications	Diploma in IT or equivalent	Certificate in Office Information Systems
Knowledge		Knowledge of the insurance industry
Specific skills and aptitudes	Ability to solve IT problems Excellent communication	Plan and deliver IT training programmes
Experience	At least two years' previous experience of general office work	Previous experience of managing IT systems
Personal attributes	Ability to form and maintain good working relationships with colleagues and clients	

• experience

• personal attributes.

The extent to which these characteristics are essential or desirable should be specified.

Competency framework   An alternative to the person specification is the competency framework. Competencies are "all the work-related personal attributes, knowledge, skills and values that a person draws upon to do their work well" as defined by Roberts (1997). Instead of designing a person specification for each job, you may prefer to draw up a framework of competencies that can be applied to all of the jobs within your organisation. The Irish Civil Service has adopted this approach and has identified seventeen competencies, such as communication skills, customer service, analytical abilities, teamwork, initiative, leadership skills and problem-solving abilities. You will need to specify the level of performance required for each competency within different job categories, as it may vary.

Figure 3.4: Sample Competency Framework for Administrator

Communication skills
Needs to be able to communicate effectively with both customers and work colleagues.

Customer service
Demonstrates the importance of managing all client enquiries promptly and courteously. Understands the need to build and maintain client relationships.

Technical expertise
Illustrates ability to manage IT systems to ensure that they are being fully utilised.

Work organisation
Is able to plan and prioritise work to meet deadlines.

Problem solving
Can investigate and analyse problems and present realistic solutions.

Foot and Hook (2002: 41) suggest that when you are designing a competency framework, you need to:

- decide whether a single framework can be applied to all employees
- select competencies relevant to your business
- choose enough competencies to represent the skills, knowledge and personal qualities required in your organisation.

The use of the competency-based approach provides an opportunity to integrate HR activities, as the competencies identified can be applied in processes such as recruitment, selection, training, appraisal and in the design of payment systems.

Terms and conditions   Examples of terms and conditions that should be explained are:

- details of hours to be worked
- holidays
- payment
- fringe benefits (such as health insurance, pension plan).

See Terms of Employment (Information) Act, 1994 and 2001 in Chapter 13.

Note When you are producing the documentation described above, you must keep the equal opportunities legislation in mind. Be careful not to discriminate against anyone because of age, sex, marital status, race, religion, sexual orientation or because they are a member of the travelling community. For more detailed explanations of equality legislation, see Chapter 13.

The External Environment

The employee profile and job analysis will help you to stay informed about the human resources currently available to you and about the jobs that exist in your organisation. You will also need to keep up to date with developments in the external environment that may have an impact on your organisation's requirements for human resources.

An analysis of the external environment can be conducted by considering the factors that may impact on your organisation. These include:

- competition
- changes in employment law
- availability of government subsidies
- fluctuations in tax, interest rates, exchange rates and inflation
- unemployment levels and trends
- changes in lifestyle and population trends
- new materials, products and processes
- availability of labour
- telecommunications and technology
- transport and infrastructure developments.

Beardwell and Holden (1997) propose that analysis of the current environment leads to the development of:

- recruitment plans – to avoid unexpected staff shortages
- training plans – to avoid skill shortages
- management development plans – to avoid managerial shortages or bottlenecks in the system
- industrial relations plans – to avoid industrial unrest resulting from changes in the quantity or quality of employees.

Forecast Demand and Supply of Labour

Once you have a clear idea of the human resources currently available, you have to prepare a forecast of future shortages and surpluses of staff and skills. In other words, you need to estimate whether you will have to increase or decrease the number or type of employees over the coming weeks and months. Predicting future human resource needs is difficult in the long term and requires a certain amount of flexibility. Early in 2001, when hotel and guesthouse owners were taking bookings for the following months and estimating the number of employees that they would need, they did not realise the impact the outbreak of foot-and-mouth disease would have on their plans. As is the case with the weather, short-term forecasts are more accurate.

In order to prepare a human resource forecast, you need to consider two aspects of the future situation. First, you have to estimate the future quantity and quality of people required, i.e. the future demand for labour. Second, you need to try to determine the number of people likely to be available both from within and outside the organisation, i.e. the supply of labour.

Demand for Labour

Demand for labour is estimated after considering:

Managerial judgement Successful planning largely depends on the experience and judgement of the manager and other key personnel in trying to predict the number and type of employees that will be needed in the future and when exactly they will be required.

Business plans Examining your organisation's plans will help you to calculate the future demand for labour. Your business plans can help you to identify whether there will be staff shortages or surpluses in the future. For example, if a new product is planned or future output is going to increase, you may need to take on more staff. Increased mechanisation or a merger with another organisation could result in staff reduction.

Past trends Analysing past trends can help you to recognise the factors influencing the demand for labour. For example, examination of seasonal variations helps to pinpoint times of the year when more staff are required. The Irish company Lir Chocolates increases its number of staff from 40 to 60 in advance of times of increased demand for chocolate such as Christmas, Valentine's Day, Mother's Day and Easter.

Supply of Labour

Besides measuring the future demand for labour, the organisation needs to estimate the availability of workers in the future. Supply of labour is calculated by examining:

Staff turnover Staff turnover needs to be measured and analysed in order to forecast future losses and to identify why staff members leave the organisation. There are a number of reasons why people leave their jobs, which include:

- job does not live up to expectations
- better pay and conditions elsewhere
- lack of flexible work arrangements
- retirement

- dismissal
- redundancy.

Understanding why people leave their jobs can help to increase staff retention. For example, if workers tend to leave because the job was not what they expected, you will have to examine your methods of recruitment and induction; if it is because better pay and conditions are offered somewhere else, then you may need to review your reward system. Retirement can be predicted by examining the employee age profile. You need to identify whether staff retention is a problem in all sections of the organisation or is concentrated in a few or just one. Reasons for staff turnover can be examined by job attitude questionnaires, exit questionnaires and by conducting exit interviews. There are a number of measurement tools available to managers, such as the turnover index and stability rate, which enable comparisons to be made from year to year.

Turnover Index

This formula is used to determine the number of employees leaving an organisation during a period (normally one year) as a percentage of the average employed during the same period.

$$\frac{\text{No. of leavers in year}}{\text{Average no. of staff in post during year}} \times 100 = \% \text{ turnover}$$

For example, if you employed an average of 150 employees for one year and during this time 6 employees left, then your turnover is 4 per cent.

$$\frac{6 \times 100}{150} = 4\%$$

Stability Rate

The stability rate reflects the percentage of employees who have at least one year's service with the organisation. This gives an indication of the organisation's effectiveness in retaining key employees.

$$\frac{\text{No. of employees with one year's service}}{\text{No. of employees employed one year ago}} \times 100 = \% \text{ stability}$$

For example, if you currently employ 140 staff, and the number of employees employed one year ago was 150, then your staff stability is 93 per cent.

$$\frac{140 \times 100}{150} = 93\%$$

The labour market   As an employer, you need to be informed of local and national employment levels and of the skill levels of those available for work. It would be unwise to plan for expansion in an area that will not be able to supply the required employees. The existence of competing organisations in the locality will also affect the availability of employees. In addition, you need to be aware of the current cost of labour in your industry. Costs include pay, benefits and PRSI, as well as the costs associated with recruitment, selection, training and the time taken for an employee to become fully effective in the job.

Devise Plans

When you have assessed the future staffing requirements of your organisation, you will have to decide how to deal with either a surplus or a shortage of workers. In the case where it seems that there will be an oversupply of workers, your options include the following:

- lay off agency staff

- ban immediate recruitment

- redeploy staff to other departments/functions

- consider offering part-time work and job-share opportunities

- introduce early retirement

- offer leave of absence

- reduce working hours

- offer redundancy (see Chapter 13 for legislation regarding redundancy).

It is important to ensure that all appropriate employment legislation is adhered to, for example The Redundancy Payments Acts, 1967–2003, The Protection of Employment Act, 1977, Unfair Dismissals Acts, 1977–1993 and Protection of Employees (Part-Time Work) Act, 2001. See Chapter 13 for further details.

Note Making employees redundant will probably be your last option. You may decide to help those being made redundant by arranging financial planning advice or counselling. Some organisations engage the services of outplacement consultants to help departing employees with CV and interview preparation. They may contact other similar organisations to see if they have any suitable vacancies for those employees being made redundant. Those who are remaining with the organisation will also need support, as they may be experiencing feelings of insecurity or even guilt as a result of the changing situation.

If forecasting indicates a future shortage of workers, plans will have to be made to try to retain current employees and recruit new ones. See Chapter 8 for advice on how to retain staff; recruitment is the subject of Chapter 4.

Implement and Review

Once you have formulated your plans, it is important that they be implemented; otherwise, there is a danger that the human resource plans will remain aspirational. This stage of the planning process should include a review of the resources and methods, as well as a timetable showing deadlines for implementation of different stages of the strategy.

It was pointed out at the beginning of this chapter that planning is a continuous process. Once HR plans are made, it does not mean that the organisation has to stick rigidly to them. HR plans are made based on information at a particular time and you will need to monitor the organisation's internal and external environments for any signs of change. You will need to review plans in light of any changes that occur in these environments.

Finally, the entire human resource planning process should be evaluated to ensure its effectiveness. You need to consider whether the sources of information you used to make your decisions were sufficiently reliable and accurate.

Chapter 4

RECRUITMENT: ATTRACTING CANDIDATES TO THE ORGANISATION

"Recruitment is the process of generating a pool of candidates from which to select the appropriate person to fill a job vacancy."

(Heery and Noon, 2001: 298)

This chapter will help you to:

- decide what to do when a vacancy arises
- plan the recruitment process
- consider different methods of recruitment
- design an advertisement
- anticipate some of the difficulties you might encounter during the recruitment process.

Recruitment and selection are major parts of the employment process. Recruitment refers to ways of attracting candidates to the organisation. This chapter looks at how to attract potential candidates and encourage them to apply for vacancies in your organisation. Selection is the part of the process where the successful candidates are chosen from those who applied. Methods of selection will be evaluated in the next chapter.

THE RECRUITMENT PROCESS

The recruitment process is linked to the overall HR plan, which in turn stems from the organisation's business plan. Therefore, it is useful for managers and supervisors to be involved in decision making at all stages of the recruitment process.

Consider the Alternatives

A job may become vacant when an employee leaves the organisation, when a new position is created due to expansion or when an employee

requests job-sharing arrangements. The first issue to be considered is
whether it is necessary to replace an employee who has left or whether
expansion requires the employment of new staff. When a job vacancy
arises in an organisation, it may not be necessary to recruit a new employee. Taking on a new worker is only one possible solution; there are
alternatives to recruitment.

Subcontracting

In some organisations, cleaning, catering and security staff are not direct
employees of the organisation. These workers are employed by
subcontractors who organise rosters, pay wages and solve staffing
problems such as absenteeism. Subcontracting is common in the building
industry and in computer programming, where people are subcontracted
to work on specific projects. By using subcontractors, you can avoid the
many employer responsibilities involved in finding and training staff. In
addition, the subcontractor carries the administrative burden of employing
staff. However, you will have little control over the subcontracted
employees.

Automation

There are situations where new technology or equipment may replace
employees. For example, the banking industry has responded to con-
sumer demand for more flexible and convenient banking hours by in-
stalling ATM machines and internet banking instead of lengthening bank
opening hours and employing more staff. Automation is common in
industries that previously required a lot of skill, such as printing and
textile production. However, this alternative to recruitment usually requires heavy financial investment.

Overtime

If you only require extra staff in the short term, you may prefer to offer
overtime work to existing employees, who might welcome the opportunity to earn extra money. Since recruitment and selection can be an expensive and time-consuming process, it might not be worth employing
someone new for a short period. However, there is a danger when offering overtime that the regular work is deliberately prolonged to create
more overtime hours. You need to remember that according to the Organisation of Working Time Act, 1997, the maximum average working
week is 48 hours. Averaging may be balanced out over a four-month
period, or for six or twelve months in certain circumstances.

Job Enrichment or Job Enlargement

Another way to manage the vacancy is to divide the workload among existing staff. Job enlargement involves combining smaller tasks into one job. Job enrichment entails giving workers more tasks to perform and more control and responsibility over how they are performed. You may have to write up new job descriptions to incorporate any extra tasks and responsibilities assigned to employees. See the section on job design in Chapter 3.

Note A decision to avoid taking on new staff by using one of the alternatives mentioned above may be met with resistance by staff and demands for higher salaries. For suggestions on how to implement change, see Chapter 10.

Review Job Description and Person Specification

Once you have decided to go ahead and recruit a new employee, you need to carry out a comprehensive examination of the vacancy. You need to know as much as possible about the job and what is expected of the individual who will fill the vacancy. This information is provided by the job analysis, which was described in Chapter 3. Now is a good time to review the job description and consider whether the job content has changed and whether the position should be offered on a full-time, part-time or contract basis. You may have to update the job description and person specification accordingly. These documents provide the starting point for the recruitment process by helping you to focus on what needs to be done and what kind of person would be best suited to the job. This information can also facilitate the design of the job advertisement and help to shape the expectations of potential applicants.

Choose Sources of Recruitment

Investing enough time and resources in the recruitment process can help you to avoid the potential negative outcomes of ineffective recruiting. If the individual selected for the job turns out to have been a poor choice, you will have to face the cost of a further search. Using inappropriate sources may mean that time and money will be wasted.

There are a number of ways you can attract people to your organisation; the source(s) you choose depends on the type of job and the availability of workers. Armstrong (1993) suggests that the criteria of cost, speed and the likelihood of providing good candidates should be considered when choosing a recruitment source.

One or more of the following sources can be utilised.

Internal Search

There may be somebody already working in your organisation who can fill the vacancy. Internal advertising may help to attract suitable applicants.

One of the strengths of this approach is that information regarding the candidate is available from personnel records and from their supervisor. Moreover, because the employee is familiar with the organisation, it is more likely that their expectations of the job will be met. This reduces the chances of a person leaving in the early stages of employment in a new job. Carl Rogers (1947) was among those writers who believe that people have a natural desire to reach their fullest potential. A policy of filling vacancies from within can therefore serve to motivate workers. Finally, this method of recruitment is fast and inexpensive.

However, searching within the organisation for someone to fill a vacancy limits the pool of potential applicants, as qualified and experienced individuals outside the company are automatically excluded from the process. Furthermore, it may be more beneficial to look outside the organisation for someone with new ideas and new ways of doing things. There is also the danger that staff that have not been selected may become demotivated. Another drawback of the internal search is that, once you have found someone within the organisation to fill the vacancy, you may have another vacancy to fill.

Previous Applicants

Even if your attempt to fill the vacancy internally is not successful, there are other fast and inexpensive ways of finding potential employees. Looking through the CVs and application forms that people have sent in recently may identify a suitable candidate. These CVs and application forms may have been received as job applications or simply by people enquiring about current vacancies. An individual who was unsuccessful in a previous application could be the right person for the job in this instance.

Recommendations

Asking current employees if they know anyone suitable could be effective. Such recommendations can be useful because the employee should be able to give a realistic description of the job and the company to the potential candidate.

While using employee recommendations to find new employees is probably most common in low-skilled jobs, this method is not confined to such work. In times of high employment, companies may turn to their highly skilled, professional employees in the hope that they have similarly qualified friends working in other organisations. Some companies offer financial incentives to their employees for making successful recommendations. However, as with the internal search, the pool of potential candidates is narrowed if previous applications and employee recommendations are relied upon.

It may be worth contacting people who have worked for the organisation in the past to see if they are interested in returning. These individuals are familiar with the organisation and how it operates. Moreover, you can easily confirm the suitability of these people by speaking to colleagues and supervisors, as well as by checking performance appraisal records.

FÁS

FÁS provides a free service to employers who wish to recruit new staff. You can contact your local FÁS office or log on to www.fas.ie for details of how to advertise.

Among the advantages of using FÁS to recruit employees are that the service is free and your job vacancy will be seen by people currently looking for work. However, the pool of potential candidates is limited to those seeking employment.

Advertising

You may decide not to confine your search for new workers to the existing workforce and their contacts. Your decision to extend the search may be made in an effort to widen the pool of potential applicants. In some cases, particularly in the public sector, there may be a legal obligation to advertise certain positions externally. This is to ensure open competition and avoid the possibility of nepotism.

Advertising the job vacancy in national newspapers or specialist magazines can be expensive, but the message reaches a larger number of potential applicants. In Ireland, the *Irish Independent* on Thursdays and *The Irish Times* on Fridays have supplements devoted to job vacancies. While these sources are commonly used to recruit professional and managerial staff, it is equally usual to find small ads in local newspapers advertising lower skilled jobs.

Jobs can also be advertised on radio jobspots, teletext and the Internet. You can advertise vacancies on your own website or on the websites of recruitment agencies such as www.irishjobs.ie, www.monster.ie, www.recruitireland.com, www.totaljobs.com and www.myjob.ie. One of the main advantages of using the Internet as a source of recruitment is that you can give more detailed information about the job than can be provided in a newspaper advertisement. In addition, your advertisement could attract applicants from all over the world.

Where you decide to place your advertisement depends on the type of job, your advertising budget, your target audience and the time available. Job advertisements have the additional benefit of increasing the organisation's public profile. You can find advice on how to design a job advertisement later in this chapter.

Recruitment Agencies

As the search for new employees can be time-consuming and requires a certain amount of skill, you may choose to engage the services of a recruitment agency. Collins McNicholas and ICE are examples of large recruitment agencies in Ireland. Such agencies are often used to find clerical and secretarial staff as well as managerial personnel. In addition, many agencies specialise in finding staff in particular industries, such as engineering, catering or IT.

You will need to ensure that the agency is clear about your staffing requirements in order to avoid the selection of unsuitable candidates. This is an expensive way of finding staff, as the agency charges a fee based on a percentage of a year's salary. A major advantage is that the recruitment process is left to professionals and this saves time and work for the organisation.

Search Consultants

Search consultants, or "head-hunters", are sometimes used for senior management positions. Search consultants have a network of contacts and can identify suitable people in other organisations. Potential candidates are approached directly and informally by the head-hunter to discuss the possibility of taking up a job elsewhere. This is probably the most expensive source of recruitment. Examples of search consultants in Ireland include Merc Partners, Amrop Hever, GMB Executive Search and Selection, and Solomon Search Partners.

Colleges and Universities

Some organisations try to identify potential employees before they graduate. Typically, representatives visit colleges once a year and present information on their organisation to final year students and advise them of job opportunities that exist. Students are encouraged to apply and training programmes are often offered to successful candidates.

One of the main advantages to the organisation of recruiting straight from college is that these new employees are likely to be up to date on the latest developments in their area of study. However, they may not have much work experience and may require training.

Recruitment Fairs

Employers can attend recruitment fairs as part of the recruitment process. At recruitment fairs, employers are invited, for a fee, to set up a stand and provide information about job opportunities in their organisations. *Opportunities 2003* at the RDS in Dublin attracted 120,000 visitors during its 4 days. Over 50 organisations offered jobs in areas such as IT, engineering, finance, insurance, sales and marketing. Christian Dior, McDonalds, Aldi, Extravision and Kerry Group are examples of companies who were represented. This recruitment fair, organised by FÁS, takes place every January or February.

Recruitment fairs put employers in contact with people who are either currently unemployed or thinking of changing jobs. Organisations who exhibit at recruitment fairs also have the opportunity to increase their public profile. The cost to the employer varies. Attending a jobs fair in a college will be relatively inexpensive but exhibiting at a major recruitment fair abroad can be quite costly.

Application Form or CV?

You need to decide how you want applicants to apply for the job. The most common forms of application are by application form or by curriculum vitae and covering letter. Applications can also be received by post or by e-mail.

The main advantage of using an application form is that you can decide in advance exactly what kind of information you are looking for and design the application form accordingly. You can have a section where the applicant can include any additional information they feel is relevant. Having a standard form for every applicant to fill in makes it easier for the recruiter to locate specific information quickly and this aids comparison of applicants at the shortlisting stage. However, you will need to allow enough time for the application form to reach the applicant by post (unless you make it available on your website) and for it to be completed and returned to the organisation.

For small organisations that need to recruit quickly and that do not have the resources available to handle a large number of enquiries, applications by CV and covering letter may be more suitable. Using this method can cut down the time between the date of advertisement and

Table 4.1: Summary of Sources of Recruitment

Method	Advantages	Disadvantages
Internal search	• applicant knows organisation and vice versa • fast • inexpensive • can help motivation	• narrows pool of applicants • organisation may need new blood • still have a vacancy to fill • may have negative effect on motivation
Previous applicants	• information on candidates already available • quick • inexpensive	• narrows pool of applicants • may no longer be available
Recommendations	• contacts made through existing employees • applicants may be familiar with organisational culture	• narrows pool of applicants • may be too similar to existing employees
FÁS	• free service • ad will be seen by people looking for work	• narrows pool of applicants
Advertising	• open competition • increases profile of organisation • large number of potential candidates	• can be expensive
Recruitment agencies	• professional recruiters • saves time for organisation	• very expensive
Search consultants	• have useful contacts • can identify suitable people	• very expensive
Colleges and Universities	• up-to-date qualifications • can be trained in way to suit organisation	• little or no work experience
Recruitment fairs	• attract interested people • increase organisation's profile	• may be expensive

the closing date for applications. CVs can provide more information than standardised application forms. The main drawback of using CVs is that you may not find the specific information you are looking for if the applicant does not include it in the CV. Moreover, comparing applications for shortlisting purposes will be more difficult than when using a standard application form. (See Appendix 1 for sample application form.)

DESIGNING THE ADVERTISEMENT

In order to avoid unwanted applications, the advertisement should be designed in such a way as to attract suitable candidates, while deterring unsuitable candidates from applying. You may decide to engage the services of a specialist advertising agency for advice and guidance on how to produce high-impact recruitment advertising. In any case, the following information should be included in the advertisement:

- company name and information about the company
- why the vacancy exists (optional)
- job title and responsibilities
- the person required
- pay and benefits (optional)
- statement of policy on issues such as equal opportunities (optional)
- how to apply
- closing date.

See Figures 4.1 and 4.2 for sample advertisements.

CONSTRAINTS ON RECRUITMENT

This section outlines some of the obstacles you may encounter when attempting to employ new workers. Recruiting new employees can be difficult if either the organisation or the profession has a bad image or reputation. Work practices or industrial relations problems may negatively influence the perception of potential applicants. During the nurses' strike in 1999, lack of career development opportunities was mentioned as one of the difficulties in attracting new nurses to the profession.

Some vacancies are difficult to fill due to the nature of the job itself. It may be perceived to be unpleasant, dangerous, badly paid or too

Figure 4.1: Sample Advertisement

Company Logo
Office Administrator

XXX is a leading provider of business solutions to the hospitality and tourism industry and has offices throughout Ireland. Due to ongoing expansion, we wish to appoint an Office Administrator at our new offices in Bray.

The successful candidate will be required to:

• provide a comprehensive office support service to ensure that an efficient administrative function is maintained

• manage all client enquiries

• undertake computer research on recent development in the hospitality and tourism industry.

The ideal candidate will have:

• a diploma in IT

• minimum three years' experience in an office environment

• excellent IT skills

• excellent communication skills.

The salary offered for this position is €____

For further information and application form, please contact:

Closing date is Friday, 5 January

XXX Limited is an equal opportunity employer

Figure 4.2: Sample Advertisement

Trainee Customer Service

Staff required by a leading financial services company in the insurance industry. These positions involve handling customer queries on all aspects of car and home insurance and processing related customer transactions. Good leaving certificate and word-processing skills an advantage.

Send CV to:

---

stressful. The hospitality industry sometimes finds it difficult to recruit and retain staff because of the unsociable working hours and poor pay.

The process of recruiting and selecting staff can be quite expensive depending on the methods used. In addition, the employer has a number of financial obligations to the new worker which may prove to be prohibitive. Apart from salary or wages, the employer is obliged to make PRSI contributions for each member of staff.

The Employment Equality Act, 1998 is legislation that obliges an employer to provide equal employment opportunities to potential candidates. This is particularly relevant today due to the increasing diversity within the workforce in terms of age, sex, race, qualifications and backgrounds. For more information on this Act, see Chapter 13.

A final word

The recruitment process takes time. Weeks may elapse between the time the job becomes vacant and the applications begin to arrive. Once you have received the applications, you have to focus your attention on selecting the appropriate candidate for the job. This part of the process is detailed in the next chapter.

Chapter 5

SELECTION: CHOOSING THE RIGHT PERSON FOR THE JOB

"Selection is the process of assessing job applicants using one or a variety of methods with the purpose of finding the most suitable person for the organisation."

(Heery and Noon, 2001: 320)

This chapter will help you to:

- work within the law when choosing someone for a job

- become familiar with the methods available for selecting employees

- adopt the appropriate selection procedure to meet your recruitment needs

- plan your selection process systematically

- plan and carry out an effective interview

- make an offer of employment

- evaluate the effectiveness of your recruitment and selection campaign.

If the recruitment campaign (Chapter 4) has been successful, there should be a number of job applications for you to consider. The next stage in the employment process involves choosing the best person.

WORKING WITHIN THE LAW

Throughout the process of selection, care must be taken not to discriminate against any candidate on the basis of age, race, gender, marital status, family status, sexual orientation, religious belief, disability or membership of the travelling community, as applicants are protected by the Employment Equality Act, 1998. Applicants are protected from discrimination with regard to recruitment advertising, employment, conditions of employment, training and promotion. When selecting candidates for employment, you must be very careful not to ask questions or make decisions that could be interpreted as discriminatory. Reference to any of the above topics in an interview situation could lead to an inference of discrimination, whether intended or not. Here are three examples of cases taken under the Employment Equality Act.

Hughes v Aer Lingus (2002)   A candidate being interviewed for a cabin crew position was asked how she would cope with younger people being in charge and how she would feel about starting at the bottom rung of the ladder. The Equality Officer found that the questions were asked in a manner as to give the complainant reason to believe that her age was an issue. The employer was ordered to pay €5,000 for the distress that the interviewee had suffered in relation to the discriminatory line of questioning and in bringing a complaint. As the performance of the candidate at interview may have suffered due to the questioning, the Equality Officer ordered that she be given an opportunity to re-interview for a cabin crew position with a different panel within twelve weeks.

Freeman v Superquinn (2002)   In March 2002, Superquinn was ordered to pay €20,000 in compensation to an employee at one of its Dublin stores who was discriminated against on the grounds of age, marital and family status when she applied for the post of head cashier. The Equality Officer found that Ms Freeman had been passed over for a promotion because she was married and had a child.

Gleeson v Rotunda and Mater Hospitals (2000)   Ms Gleeson is a doctor who was asked at an interview about the time she "had her babies". The job went to someone who she considered less qualified. She won her case in the Labour Court on the grounds of gender discrimination and was awarded €63,500.

METHODS OF SELECTION

There are many criteria for choosing the right person for a job. A manager in a large multinational company based in Ireland recounted a situation where a candidate was taken out to lunch by his prospective employers. It was quickly decided that he would not be offered the job because he had put salt on his food before tasting it!

There are a number of more conventional methods available for selecting a person to fill a job vacancy. The interview tends to be the central selection method but is often supplemented by one or more of the other selection techniques.

Shortlisting

Shortlisting is a stage between recruitment and selection and is necessary in situations where a large number of applications are received. Shortlisting involves reducing the applications to a more manageable number by narrowing down the field of applicants who will continue to the next stage of the selection process. Two methods of shortlisting are outlined below.

Method 1

Take a copy of the person specification or competency framework (Chapter 3) and compare it against the curriculum vitae or application form of each candidate to decide whether they meet the requirements of the job. You could do this by putting a plus sign (+) beside the knowledge, skills and qualities that the candidate possesses and a minus sign (–) beside those that the candidate is lacking. If you are not sure, or cannot yet make an assessment on a particular skill, insert a question mark (?). Eliminate candidates who do not possess the criteria deemed as "essential" in the person specification or competency framework.

Method 2

Look at the job description or competency framework and give points for each criterion that the candidate meets. Add up the points and eliminate the lowest ranking candidates.

Whichever method you use, it is important that you focus on relevant information. Remember that the aim of the selection process is to obtain the best match for the job. If possible, two people should independently draw up a shortlist and discuss their choices before making a final decision. It is important to be consistent and systematic during the shortlisting process.

The shortlisting exercise should result in the compilation of two lists: those who will continue to the next stage of the selection process and those who will not.

Candidates who will Continue to the Next Stage of the Selection Process

These candidates should be contacted and given details of date, time and place of the interview and the name(s) of those interviewing. If the candidates are required to carry out any tests, they should be notified at this stage. If you wish to see confirmation of qualifications, ask candidates to bring this with them to the interview. (See Appendix 2 for sample letter.)

Candidates who are not Suitable

As a matter of courtesy, candidates considered unsuitable for this position should be contacted and advised that their applications have been unsuccessful on this occasion. You may wish to keep their details on file. (See Appendix 3 for sample letter.)

The Selection Interview

An interview, however informal, is part of almost every selection process. There are many reasons for its popularity.

* It provides an opportunity for the manager to meet the potential employee face-to-face.

* Most of us have a tendency to trust our own intuition and believe that we are good judges of character, so the prospect of employing someone without ever meeting them seems foolish.

* It provides an opportunity for the interviewer to obtain information about the candidates, communicate information about the job and clarify applicants' questions.

* It can be carried out almost anywhere and no special equipment is required.

* It is usually faster and cheaper than methods such as psychological testing.

* It is suitable for selecting people into all types of jobs.

Although it is the most popular way to choose people for jobs, evidence (for example Reilly and Chao, 1982) suggests that the interview is not always the best method of predicting future performance at work. Quite often, interviewers have had little training in interviewing techniques and may underestimate some of the limitations of perception and memory. Some possible reasons why the interview is such a poor predictor of future performance are:

• the interviewer does not prepare in advance

• the interview has no structure

• the questions asked do not relate to the job

• the interviewer has problems remembering candidates' responses

- the perceptual limitations of the interviewer
- the interviewer talks too much.

The Interview Process

The following guidelines will help you to get the most out of the interview process and avoid the pitfalls mentioned above.

Before the Interview

There are a number of things you should do before the interview takes place.

1. *Read the application form or CV and match it against the job description and person specification*
   The average interview lasts for approximately 30 to 40 minutes. This does not give you much time to get to know the candidate or to decide whether the individual is suitable for the job. You need to prepare beforehand in order to make best use of the interview time. You should read the application form carefully and match the candidate's details against the job description and the person specification. Preparation of this kind is essential, as it gives you the opportunity to identify aspects of the application that need to be explored or clarified during the course of the interview. If you are inadequately prepared, you may miss some important pieces of information and make a decision based on insufficient or irrelevant information.

2. *Design the structure of the interview*
   The interview should have an opening, middle and a closing. The objectives of the opening stage are to:

   - welcome the interviewee
   - make introductions
   - establish rapport and put the candidate at their ease
   - explain the purpose and the structure of the interview.

   The main aims of the middle part are to:

   - ask relevant questions
   - provide information to the candidate about the organisation, the job and the terms and conditions of employment.

The closing stage should be used to:

* give the candidate an opportunity to ask questions and clarify any outstanding issues
* ask the candidate if they feel they have had a fair interview
* allow both the candidate and interviewer to make any final comments
* thank the candidate for attending
* inform the candidate of what happens next in the selection process.

3. *Think about the questions you are going to ask*
   You need to make decisions about what questions you are going to ask the candidates. It is fairer to ask the same questions to each candidate and it makes it easier to compare candidates' responses later. It is important to allow for a certain amount of flexibility, too. Sticking rigidly to the list of questions may mean that certain interesting points made during the interview are not followed up. Keep in mind the employment equality legislation and do not ask questions that may be interpreted as discriminatory.

   There are three styles of interview. The first style is the traditional interview, which goes through the education and work experience of the candidate with the aim of building up a picture of what the person is like. For example, a candidate might be asked why they chose a certain career or course of study. The problem with this style of interviewing is that the information obtained during the interview is not enough on its own to predict the individual's future performance at work.

   The second style of interviewing involves describing typical situations or problems that the candidate may experience in the job and asking the candidate how they would handle them. For example, a sales assistant could be asked how they would deal with an angry customer making a complaint. While this style of interviewing provides an indication of how the candidate might deal with certain situations in theory, it does not guarantee how situations would be handled in practice.

   The third style of interviewing is based on the assumption that evidence of past performance and behaviour is the best predictor of future performance and behaviour. Candidates are asked to describe how they dealt with particular situations in the past. The questions asked in this type of interview are chosen very carefully (with the help of the competency framework or person specification discussed in Chapter 3) to ensure that they relate to the competencies relevant for the job. If a job requires good decision-making skills, the candidate could be asked to give a specific example of how they arrived at a particular work-related decision. The main drawback of this approach is that the preparation is time-consuming and interviewers need training in the technique.

Whatever style or mixture of styles is chosen, it is important that the questions asked are relevant to the job and to candidates' ability to do the job. Otherwise, an unsuitable candidate could be chosen.

4. *Choose a venue and room layout*
A candidate will form an impression of your organisation on entering your premises. Ensure that the reception area is clean and tidy and that there is someone available to greet candidates. Choose a quiet, private room and make sure that you will not be disturbed. Decide how to arrange the table and chairs in the room. Having the interviewer sit behind a desk with the interviewee opposite creates an air of formality, which may be what the candidate expects. For a more informal setting, the desk can be removed or chairs can be arranged at right angles to each other.

During the Interview

1. *Take notes*
Even after a short interview, it can be difficult to remember the answers that candidates gave to each question asked. When a number of candidates have been interviewed, it is even more difficult to remember what each person said at the end of the day. This is why it is important to make notes of candidates' responses during the interview or immediately afterwards. At a panel interview, when one member of the panel is asking questions, another can record the answers given.

2. *Be aware of perceptual limitations*
Most people have a need to make sense of other people, situations and what is going on around them. There is a tendency to satisfy this need with very little information. The perceptual errors discussed below have one thing in common: they all reflect efforts to evaluate people and situations based on either inadequate or irrelevant information. The interviewer must realise that perceptual abilities are limited and that because of this errors are made when evaluating other people. Trained interviewers are aware of these tendencies and can try to reduce their effects.

Stereotyping occurs when we try to categorise people according to characteristics such as age, sex, address, education, school attended, accent, race and so on. The problem is that we should not jump to conclusions about people based on this kind of information. We cannot assume that all old people are resistant to change or that all people living in a certain area are wealthy. It is particularly important that interviewers become aware of their biases, as there is legislation in place to ensure equal opportunities and protect people from discrimination. *Do not allow yourself to make judgements based on irrelevant information.*

The *halo effect* is a tendency to focus on one positive character-istic of the candidate and to generalise and assume the candidate has other positive characteristics. An example of this would be noticing that the interviewee has achieved very high academic standards and assuming that they will reach high standards of performance in the workplace, too. The *horns effect* is the tendency to generalise from one negative characteristic. *Do not make judgements based on in-sufficient information.*

People have a tendency to focus more at the beginning of things and to remember the start better. This is called the *primacy effect*. Since people feel they need to understand situations, even if they only have sketchy information to help them reach their conclusions, they tend to make judgements quite quickly based on early informa-tion. If this happens at an interview, added to the fact that we trust our own intuition, the interviewer is likely to make a decision on a candidate right at the start and try to justify this initial decision for the duration of the interview. *Do not make judgements too quickly.*

There is also a danger that the interviewer's judgement of a candidate will be influenced by the performance of the previous candidate. This is called the *contrast effect* and implies that if the previous candidate is excellent, the next will not be seen to be as good as they really are. Similarly, if the first candidate performs badly, the next candidate can appear better than they really are. *Try to evaluate candidates on their own merits, not in comparison with the previous interviewee.*

3. *Do not dominate the interview*
Untrained and inexperienced interviewers sometimes do most of the talking during the interview. Ideally, the interviewee should speak for at least 80 per cent of the interview time. The corollary of this is that the interviewer should be listening for 80 per cent of the time. The interviewer needs to be able to concentrate on what the candidate is saying in order to take in as much information as possible. A good interviewer can formulate questions that encourage the candidate to speak freely.

- *Open questions* begin with words such as "tell me about", "what", "why", "how", "who" or "when" and cannot be answered with just "yes" or "no".

- *Probing questions* can be used to follow up on answers already given.

- *Hypothetical questions* help the interviewer to test creativity with questions such as "What would you do if...?"

To find out about a candidate's ability to work with other people or as part of a team, you could ask:

- "What do you find are the main challenges in working with other people?"

- "Can you give me an example of a situation where you found someone difficult to work with?"

- "How did you deal with the situation?"

- "What was the outcome?"

- "What would you do if a colleague was not pulling their weight within the team?"

To find out how a candidate might cope with deadlines, you could ask:

- "How do you structure your work to ensure that you meet tight deadlines?"

- "Tell me about a time when you were under pressure to meet a deadline."

- "On reflection, would you do anything differently?"

- "What would you do if a colleague phoned in sick on the day of an important deadline?

If you want to assess a candidate's ability to make decisions, ask questions such as:

- "Can you give me an example of a tough decision that you have had to make?"

- "What was the outcome of that decision?"

- "What did you learn from this experience?"

To help evaluate a candidate's ability to manage change, you could ask:

- "What action did you take to ensure that the new system was effectively introduced?"

- "How did you overcome resistance to change?"

- "What would you do if your subordinates refused to accept a change you wished to implement?"

In order to investigate a candidate's level of work motivation, you might like to ask:

- "What particular aspects of your job do you enjoy/dislike?"

4. *Use a panel*
   Using a panel to select an employee is fairer than the one-to-one approach, as selection is based on the opinions of more than one interviewer. This reduces the effects of interviewer bias and subjectivity. Panel members may have different areas of expertise, all relevant to the position. It could be that a number of people have a vested interest in the new post holder and so their involvement in the selection process is required.
   Finding a date and time to suit all panel members may be difficult. Moreover, while using a panel could lead to better decision making, there is always the danger that a dominant panel member could influence other panel members in their evaluations of candidates.

After the Interview

1. *Evaluate the information and reach a decision*
   To ensure that the information collected during the interview is evaluated objectively, it is a good idea to devise a scoring system, either for the answers to interview questions or for the items on the person specification. More marks can be allocated to more important questions. Add up the marks for each candidate and rank them from most suitable to least suitable.

2. *Keep a written record*
   You should keep a record of all interviews conducted, the procedures followed and justification for selecting the successful candidate for the following reasons:

   - to provide feedback to candidates who request it under the Freedom of Information Act, 1997

• to present evidence of a fair procedure should a candidate decide
  to pursue a case under the Employment Equality Act, 1998.

The next section outlines some of the other methods used either on their
own or as part of the selection process.

Psychological Testing

Psychological tests (also known as psychometric tests) assess
characteristics that are related to satisfactory job performance. They add
objectivity and fairness to the selection process and measure some factors
that cannot be assessed through the application form and the interview.
All candidates do the same tests under the same conditions and responses
are scored impartially. Many of the psychological tests used in the
selection process have been researched extensively and special training
is required to administer and interpret them. Psychological testing is
applicable in all kinds of job situations and costs vary depending on the
particular test. Psychological tests are used in conjunction with other
selection methods, such as the interview, and should not be used on
their own to determine suitability for a position.

Types of Psychological Tests

Intelligence tests are used as a means of selecting people for jobs in the
belief that a certain amount of intelligence is needed for job success.
The logic follows that these tests can identify those who are not smart
enough to do the job. Critics of intelligence tests claim that the tests are
biased in favour of white, middle-class people. Some research seems to
indicate that minority candidates score lower on intelligence tests than
non-minority candidates. Another criticism is that it is difficult to predict future performance based on intelligence.

Aptitude tests are designed to measure the potential an individual
has to do a particular job. Aptitude and ability tests are most suited for
jobs where specific and measurable skills are required. They are useful
for shortlisting from a large number of candidates. Aptitude tests are
particularly suitable for selecting trainees and apprentices or when introducing a new computerised system.

Personality tests are used to measure certain personality traits and
predict work behaviour. Some of the personality characteristics measured include levels of extroversion/introversion, emotional stability,
agreeableness, conscientiousness and openness. Personality tests may
be appropriate when the job involves a lot of interpersonal contact or
when certain personality characteristics are important for the job. However, those who criticise the use of personality tests in selection doubt

the stability of personality over time and question the predictive value of these tests.

More organisations are using psychological testing as part of the selection procedure. Use of psychological tests should be restricted to reputable tests, administered and interpreted only by properly trained staff. Psychological tests are available from SHL (Ireland) www.shlgroup.com/ie and ETC Consult.

Work Samples

Work samples are designed to be a sample of the behaviour performed on the job. The employers can observe the candidate's level of competency on a particular task and the candidate has the opportunity to experience the kind of work they will be doing if their application is successful. Obvious examples include a typing test and a driving test, but work samples could also involve asking the candidate to assemble a component or use a piece of equipment.

Work samples are job relevant and are more appropriate for selecting people with a trade, such as a plumber, carpenter or electrician, where there is one best way to complete a task. They are less well suited to jobs that involve working with people, such as social workers, where there may be a number of ways of dealing with a situation. This method can be quite expensive and creating a work sample can be time-consuming. Work samples are usually administered individually, which requires more time.

Situational Exercises

These are sometimes referred to as white-collar work samples. Situational exercises are used most frequently to select people for administrative and managerial jobs. An example of a situational exercise is the *In-Tray Exercise*. Candidates are given samples of work that they could expect to find in the "in-tray" on their desks and asked to deal with them. This could include writing memos, making phone calls, preparing reports and letters, prioritising and decision making. Situational exercises are job relevant and can give a good indication of a candidate's likely performance on the job. This method of selection is quite time-consuming.

References

It is common practice for organisations to seek either written or oral references for potential employees. The purpose of the reference is to obtain information relating to the candidate's employment history. The type of information sought will include:

- period of employment
- position
- salary or wages
- number of days absent
- would employer re-employ?

The source of this information is usually the candidate's current or previous employer.

It is general practice to approach previous employers earlier in the selection process and current employers at the final stage. Contacting current employers in the early stages of the selection process may jeopardise the candidate's career if the current employer is unaware that they are seeking alternative employment. Before seeking references, it is important that you obtain the candidate's permission. The decision regarding when to obtain references varies from organisation to organisation. Some organisations like to protect candidates' confidentiality and will only seek references if they are proposing to make a job offer. Alternatively, a job offer may be made subject to receipt of satisfactory references.

Using references as part of the selection procedure is inexpensive but it is difficult to know how fair it is. In many cases, candidates choose their own referees and it is unlikely that they would ask someone who would give them a bad reference. Moreover, employers may be hesitant to disclose negative information on previous employees for fear of legal action. (See Appendix 4 for sample reference request form.)

EVALUATING METHODS OF SELECTION

To help you to decide which method(s) of selection to use, you may like to consider the following criteria.

- *Validity* – does the method measure what it is supposed to measure? In other words, does an intelligence test really test intelligence?

- *Reliability* – does the method produce the same result every time? Does the method produce the same result if carried out by different people?

- *Fairness* – is this method unbiased towards different subgroups of applicants, for example race, sex?

- *Applicability* – can this method be used for many job types?

* *Cost* – is it expensive?
* *Acceptability* – is this method acceptable to both the candidate and the employer?

Table 5.1: Summary of Selection Methods*

Method	Validity	Reliability	Fairness	Applica-bility	Cost	Accepta-bility
Interview	can be low; depends on standard of interview	low	moderate	high	moderate –low	high
Intelligence tests	moderate	high	moderate	high	low	moderate
Aptitude tests	moderate	high	high	moderate	low	high
Personality tests	moderate	moderate	high	low	moderate	moderate
Work samples	high	high	high	low	high	high
Situational exercises	moderate	unknown	unknown	low	moderate	high
References	low	questionable	unknown	high	low	high

*This table is based on the work of Muchinsky (1986)

MAKING AN OFFER OF EMPLOYMENT

Under the Terms of Employment (Information) Act, 1994 and 2001, an employer must provide employees with a written statement of the particulars of the employee's terms of employment within two months of the date of commencement of employment, even if the employee ceases employment during that period.

Information to be included in the written statement is:

* the full names of the employer and employee
* the address of the employer
* the place of work
* job title or nature of the work
* date of commencement of employment
* if the contract is for a fixed term, the date on which the contract expires

- details of pay
- terms and conditions
- period of notice.

This statement must be signed by both the employer and employee, and the employer is obliged to keep the statement during the period of employment and for a further year following cessation of employment.

The Department of Enterprise, Trade and Employment provides forms that can be used for this purpose.

EVALUATING THE EFFECTIVENESS OF THE RECRUITMENT AND SELECTION PROCESS

Once the successful candidate has been appointed, it would be useful for you to assess how effective the overall recruitment and selection process has been. You can use this information to help you make decisions about any vacancies that may arise in the future. Consider the following questions:

- Was the medium used appropriate for the category of job being advertised?

- Did the advertisement (or other approach) generate sufficient quantity and quality of candidates?

- Was the exercise (advertising, postage, staff time to shortlist, test, interview etc.) cost-effective?

- Were you able to appoint someone?

- Could anything be done differently the next time to improve the recruitment and selection process?

The long-term effectiveness of your recruitment and selection campaign will only be determined by ongoing assessment of the candidate's performance in the job.

Part III

MANAGING PERFORMANCE

Chapter 6

TRAINING: DEVELOPING YOUR STAFF

"Training is the process of changing the skills, attitudes
and knowledge of employees with the purpose of improving their level of competence."

(Heery and Noon, 2001: 372)

This chapter will help you to:

- understand the importance of training and development in the
  organisation

- examine the factors that influence an organisation's training and
  development policy

- design a training and development programme

- examine different techniques used for training and development

- evaluate the training process and its impact on performance

- organise an induction training programme.

THE IMPORTANCE OF TRAINING AND DEVELOPMENT

Your organisation's most valuable resource is its employees, who can
be the key to competitive advantage. Owners and managers must ensure
that employees are equipped to meet the present and future demands in
an ever-changing competitive environment. Training and development
activities should be linked to business objectives and this requires the
involvement of all key personnel. Some of the reasons for training and
development are to:

- produce quality goods in shorter time

- improve customer service

- comply with Health and Safety regulations

- obtain or retain a quality standard such as ISO 9000 or Q Mark

- introduce new technology

- facilitate change
- retain good employees
- increase motivation
- meet employees' needs
- create and sustain an effective management team.

TRAINING AND DEVELOPMENT POLICY

Organisations' attitudes to training and development differ. The policy of some organisations is to avoid training their employees as they see it as an unnecessary expense. At the other end of the spectrum is the "learning organisation", where training and development is viewed as having an important role in improving organisational performance and is allocated the necessary resources. Many organisations, however, are willing to invest in training if it adds to competitive advantage, addresses an immediate problem or provides a financial payback.

An organisation's training policy is influenced by the following considerations:

The Labour Market

If there are not enough suitably trained people available in the labour market, then the organisation will have no choice but to provide the training itself. There is less pressure on an organisation to provide training when skilled labour is available or can be poached from other organisations.

Available Resources

Training and development can require time, money, space, equipment and qualified trainers. It is easier to become a learning organisation when these resources are available. Lack of necessary resources may force an organisation to reduce or eliminate plans for training and development.

Management Trends

Current trends suggest that organisations are shifting their style more towards HRM. This will lead companies to develop and support a learning environment.

Employment Legislation

An organisation may be legally obliged to provide certain training. For example, in the construction industry, specific training under health and safety legislation is a legal requirement. Health and Safety legislation states that every organisation must prepare a safety statement and take steps to deal with any risks or hazards in the workplace. Training needs to be provided to ensure that employees can identify dangers at work and know how to operate dangerous equipment and machinery. See Chapter 13 for more details of employment legislation.

DESIGNING A TRAINING AND DEVELOPMENT PROGRAMME

Training and development programmes can be costly and outcomes are often difficult to measure. However, owners and managers have to balance the costs associated with providing training against the cost of not providing training, which could mean the difference between success and failure for an organisation. Therefore, it is necessary that every effort is made to ensure that the training provided meets the needs of the organisation and its employees, and is cost-effective. The training cycle provides a framework to identify training needs, design a training programme, and deliver and evaluate the programme.

Figure 6.1: The Training Cycle

Identify training needs

Evaluate training programme   Design training programme

Deliver training programme

Identify Training Needs

A training need is the "gap" between desired performance and actual performance. The first stage in the training and development process is to carry out a needs analysis to assess what kind of training or development is required in the organisation. Training may be needed when you:

- *Take on a new employee.* Good training is imperative in the early stages of employment to ensure that employees settle into the organisation and become effective as soon as possible.

- *Examine the quantity and quality of work.* You may find that quality is not up to the required standard or that the quantity of goods produced can be increased.

- *Carry out an appraisal.* These assessments of employees' work performance may indicate training needs.

- *Introduce new technology.* Employees will have to learn how to use any new technology installed in the workplace. Manufacturers may provide training as part of their agreement with the organisation.

- *Establish new work practices.* Employees may require training to become familiar with new methods and processes.

- *Respond to changes in legislation.* In some cases, it may be possible to obtain funding to undertake training. The Equality Authority currently provides grants to pay for expert advice on how to put equality policies in place or on how to develop and implement equality training (see www.equality.ie).

- *Talk to employees.* You may discover that there are more appropriate and cost-effective methods of getting the job done which can be remedied with some training.

- *Examine the organisation's plans.* Any future developments such as the provision of a new service or introduction of a new product will have implications for training and developing employees.

Design the Training Programme

You will need to:

1. *Ensure organisational support for the programme.* This is necessary because training can interrupt workers' daily routines and the support and co-operation of managers and workers are important factors in the success or failure of the programme. You might find it easier to get organisational support if training takes place outside of working hours.

2. *Set specific objectives.* The specific objectives to be attained through the training and development programme should be established at the outset, as these will be used to evaluate whether or not the training

and development programme has been successful. If the training is being provided externally, these objectives can be agreed with the provider.

Figure 6.2: Examples of Specific Objectives

Upon completion of training programme, trainees will be able to, for example:

- operate a cash register

- compile a spreadsheet

- assemble a piece of equipment

- close a sale.

3. *Allocate the necessary resources.* Resources include people who are qualified to carry out the training, as well as the necessary equipment, money and space.

4. *Assist the transfer of learning.* When training is completed, participants must have the opportunity to transfer their new skills as soon as possible. Equipment used during training should be similar to the equipment used on the job. If possible, ease the pressure of work for trainees for a short time after returning to work to give them a chance to practise their new skills.

Deliver the Training Programme

There are a number of training methods available to managers.

Demonstration

Demonstration is a commonly used training technique. A supervisor or colleague shows the trainee how to do the job and then lets them do it. This method is sometimes called "Sitting next to Nellie". This is an inexpensive method of training and there is a high transfer of learning, as the trainee actively participates in the training process. In addition, the trainee is learning within the organisation from someone who actually does the job.

The problem with this method is that there is usually no structure in the procedure and it may turn out to be a time-consuming way of training the employee. Quite often, the colleague who demonstrates does not have any training skills and so may not be able to explain well how to do certain things or why they are done. In fact, the individual chosen to demonstrate to the trainee might resent having to do so and see it as an inconvenience that delays their own work. The trainee may pick up their colleague's bad habits such as taking shortcuts and not following procedures correctly. In addition, the feedback from a colleague may not be constructive.

Note It may be preferable to stagger training over a period rather than deliver it over one or two days. This will help to avoid overloading the trainee with too much information at once and will allow you to monitor the trainee's progress and rectify mistakes early on.

Coaching

Coaching is a technique usually used for trainees in managerial or supervisory positions. Planned meetings take place between the trainee and their immediate manager where the trainee can be given guidance on how to deal with situations. It often involves a certain amount of delegation of responsibility from the superior to the trainee. Such an approach to training is job relevant, as the trainee is being guided in carrying out the duties of the job. However, unless it is properly planned as part of the training process, pressures of time on the part of the superior may limit the amount of individual attention that can be given.

Mentoring

Mentoring bears a number of similarities to coaching. However, whereas the coach tends to be the individual's immediate superior, the mentor is usually a more senior manager and not always in the same area of responsibility. Coaching is one aspect of mentoring. Gibb and Megginson (1993) identified four mentoring roles:

* helping to improve performance
* helping career development
* acting as a counsellor
* sharing knowledge.

This method of management development is useful for preparing potential managers for a future role. This is known as succession planning. However, establishing a formal mentoring programme may be difficult due to the amount of time and effort involved on the part of the mentor. It may not be easy to find a manager with mentoring skills and the commitment required.

Job Rotation

Job rotation is a training technique that involves moving people from job to job or department to department to broaden their experience. It is more often used with management trainees. Job rotation is an inexpensive method of job training and it gives the trainee the opportunity to acquire knowledge and skills in different parts of the department or organisation. For this type of training to be successful it is important that a programme is designed which specifies what the trainee is expected to learn at each placement. Otherwise, this method can lack direction and prove inefficient.

Courses

Employees can be sent on courses for training and development. These courses can be designed specifically for the needs of the organisation; they may take place internally or employees may be sent to classes run by computer training centres, management institutes and so on. Designing internal courses requires the participation of key personnel as well as the training specialist to ensure that the objectives are clear and the content is appropriate. A typical example of an internal training course would be to train employees on a new piece of equipment or machinery.

Since external courses are usually not designed with a particular organisation in mind, transfer of learning to the workplace may be difficult. External courses usually provide a broad range of knowledge, not all of which may be relevant to the organisation. One of the strengths of external courses is that they can lead to making contacts with others in the same business. Both internal and external courses can be expensive.

Open or Distant Learning

Open or distant learning enables trainees to learn from material prepared and presented elsewhere. The biggest advantage for the trainee is that they can study in their own time, in their own home and at their own pace. Depending on the course, the trainee might have little contact with tutors or other students and will need to be self-motivated and dedicated. Furthermore, the content of the course needs to be examined to ensure it meets the needs of the organisation. These courses are usually quite expensive.

Workshops

This method of training is particularly suitable for managers, as it involves active discussion and problem solving. Workshops bring together a group of people who have knowledge or experience of a job with a facilitator who may be a member of management or an outside consultant. Participants often have to do a certain amount of preparation before the workshop takes place. Because the content is relevant, there can be high transfer of learning. Managing a workshop requires a trained facilitator to ensure the effectiveness of the exercise.

E-learning

E-learning techniques can include computer-based, technology-based and web-based training and learning (Foot and Hook, 2002). E-learning may be used to complement some of the methods already mentioned, such as open or distant learning. Support can be provided by chatrooms, discussion groups and on-line tutoring. Participants can work from home and have a certain amount of flexibility but they must have access to the appropriate technology.

Table 6.1: Sample Training Programme for Housekeeping Assistant in Small Hotel

Objective
Upon completion of this training programme, trainee will be able to clean and prepare bedrooms for occupancy by guests.
Duration of training Two days
Training method   Demonstration
Training provided by Housekeeper

Training content:

Task	*Description*
Bed making	Change linen, neat corners, no creases
Bathroom	Clean sink, bath, toilet, mirror, empty bin
Floors	Vacuum bedroom, wash bathroom floor
Polishing	All woodwork, furniture and windowsills
Replenishing stocks	Soap, toilet paper, towels, tea and coffee
Time Allowed	Three rooms per hour

Evaluation
Employee observes housekeeper and then carries out tasks. Progress will be evaluated by housekeeper.

Evaluate Training Programme

This stage of the training process involves evaluating whether the training and development has achieved its objectives. It is important that you

Table 6.2: Summary of Training Methods

Method	*Strengths*	*Weaknesses*
Demonstration	• inexpensive • job relevant • high transfer of learning • trainer knows the job well	• may be time-consuming • trainer may lack training skills • trainee may pick up bad habits
Coaching	• job relevant • trainer knows the job	• may lack structure • pressures of time on supervisor
Mentoring	• learn from experienced manager • useful for succession planning	• requires a lot of manager's time and effort • manager may not have mentoring skills
Job rotation	• inexpensive • trainee sees many aspects of department or organisation	• may lack structure
Courses	• professional trainers • useful for specific knowledge of skills	• expensive • transfer of learning may be low, especially with external courses • may not be job relevant
Open/distant learning	• flexibility for trainees	• expensive • requires commitment and discipline • course may not be relevant
Workshops	• job relevant	• requires advance preparation on part of participants
E-Learning	• flexibility for trainees	• requires appropriate technology

evaluate the training process, as this will help you to decide whether a particular method should be used again and how it can be implemented most effectively.

Levels of Evaluation

Kirkpatrick (1959) suggests that evaluation procedures should consider four levels of criteria: reaction, learning, behaviour and results.

Reaction The simplest way to evaluate a training and development programme is to find out what the participants thought of it. A certain amount of this information can be gauged during the training programme by monitoring facial expressions and by assessing the level of trainee participation. Trainee reaction is commonly measured by having trainees complete a questionnaire at the end of the training procedure. It is important that the items on the questionnaire reflect the objectives of the training. This information is easy to collect and, when it comes to deciding whether to repeat the programme, it is useful to know which parts of the programme participants enjoyed or disliked.

The problem with this level of evaluation is that it does not evaluate whether participants actually learned anything. Nor does it examine whether the new skills are being applied at work. In addition, information collected in this way can be subjective in nature and there is a danger that reaction measures are simply indicators of how much people liked the instructor or enjoyed the course. Enjoyment does not necessarily result in learning, though a training course that participants do not enjoy is unlikely to be repeated often.

Learning The next level of evaluating a training programme is to find out whether participants learned any new skills or information. You can do this by testing or examining trainees to see what they have learned. It is important that the test relates to the objectives of the training programme. To ensure that learning occurred *during* training, and not beforehand, it may be appropriate to test trainees before the training as well as after so that results can be compared. Testing is a more objective method of evaluation than measuring the reactions of participants.

While this method of evaluation assesses the level of learning that has been achieved, it does not measure transfer of learning. In other words, it does not assess whether skills learned during training are being applied in the workplace and it cannot be assumed that learning always translates into behavioural changes.

Behaviour This level of evaluation involves measuring job performance. This can be done by observing the trainee in the workplace both before and after training takes place and using either a checklist for specific job behaviours or a rating scale to assess to what extent certain job behaviours are evident. Whatever on-the-job performance measures are used, they should be related to the objectives of the training programme. Transfer of learning can be difficult to assess in some jobs, particularly at management level.

Results This level of evaluation attempts to relate the results of the training programme to organisational objectives. Some results that could be examined include costs, reduction in customer complaints, turnover, absenteeism, grievances and morale. However, it may not be realistic to link training directly to any of these, as there are so many other factors involved.

Unfortunately, the evaluation phase of the training–development process is often omitted. There are a number of possible reasons why. It is very difficult to evaluate whether training was successful if training objectives were not established at the outset. To assess the worth of a particular method, comparisons need to be made between the standards and behaviours before the training and those after. Without the support of top management, evaluation is often omitted from the process. It is often felt that enough money has been spent on the training itself and that the further costs of evaluation are unnecessary. Another reason why evaluation is often ignored is that the trainer may lack the skills required to carry out an evaluation. Moreover, evaluating a training–development programme may indicate that it was not effective. The risk of such an outcome may prevent evaluation taking place.

INDUCTION TRAINING

Induction is the process of introducing the employee to their new work environment. Most people are a little anxious on their first day in a new job and it is important that there is a procedure in place to help the new worker become familiar with their surroundings.

Hill and Trist (1955) found that people are most likely to leave a job in the first few weeks of employment. They called this initial period the "induction crisis" and maintained that the reasons people were more likely to leave during this time included the job not being what they expected or not liking the job.

Induction training is important because it helps to:

- create a favourable image of the organisation in the mind of the new employee
- lessen anxiety
- reduce misunderstandings
- reduce labour turnover
- achieve performance standards quickly.

Induction actually begins before a new employee starts work, as they have started to form an impression of the organisation from information sent to them as well as from the selection process they have completed. With increasing diversity in the workforce, the Labour Court has recommended that companies employing non-nationals recognise the difficulties that may arise, provide proper induction courses and make resources available to deal with social or cultural differences that may present.

All new employees should receive in written form:

• a description of the organisation

• details of pay and conditions

• a description of duties and responsibilities

• grievance procedures

• disciplinary procedures.

In addition, the induction should include:

• a tour of the workplace

• introductions to colleagues and supervisors

• an opportunity for the new employee to ask questions.

In the first days and weeks, the new employee should be monitored to make sure that they have settled in and to identify any problems at an early stage.

Chapter 7

PERFORMANCE APPRAISAL: EVALUATING EMPLOYEES' PERFORMANCE

> Performance appraisal can be defined as "a systematic approach to evaluating employees' performance, characteristics or potential with a view to assisting with decisions in a wide range of areas such as pay, promotion, employee development and motivation."
>
> (Gunnigle, Heraty and Morley, 1997: 145)

This chapter will help you to:

- understand the purposes of assessing employee work performance
- evaluate the different methods of performance appraisal
- consider who should carry out performance appraisals
- conduct an effective appraisal interview.

PURPOSES OF PERFORMANCE APPRAISAL

Performance appraisal is part of the overall HR strategy and information obtained is useful for a number of reasons. Performance appraisal will help you to:

- identify training needs
- assess the potential of current employees for future promotion
- communicate with employees by providing an opportunity for two-way feedback
- keep a record of each employee's performance at work
- make decisions regarding salary increases.

APPRAISAL METHODS

Appraisal takes place every day on an informal basis when supervisors, colleagues and customers observe and evaluate employees in the process of carrying out their duties. Nevertheless, it is important to establish a formal appraisal system that is understood and accepted by those involved. In this section, a number of appraisal methods will be described and evaluated. Performance appraisal often involves the use of more than one of these methods. Whichever methods you choose, it is essential when evaluating an employee's work that performance is compared against the requirements outlined in the job description and person specification or competency framework (see Chapter 3).

The Essay

The appraiser writes a free-form narrative and includes a description of the employee's strengths, weaknesses, potential and areas for improvement. The advantages of this method are that it is simple and flexible: the appraiser does not need any special training to carry out this type of performance evaluation and can include any information that they feel is relevant. It is possible to use great detail, which provides qualitative data.

The main drawback of the essay is that because there is no structure in this method, it will be difficult to compare employees who have been appraised in this way. In addition, the appraisal may depend on the writing skills of the appraiser. In any one organisation there may be a number of appraisers, all with different levels of writing skills, thus further confounding the issue of comparison. This method can be subjective and there is a danger with a free-form appraisal that the appraiser may focus on the employee's personality rather than on their behaviour.

The essay is probably most useful in an organisation with few employees, where the same individual carries out all of the appraisals, and for jobs where specific job behaviours are difficult to define, such as managerial positions.

Critical Incident

This method focuses on specific job behaviours. The appraiser keeps a regular account of incidences of effective and ineffective work behaviours for each employee and uses these to assess performance. An example of "good" work behaviour for a cashier might be "checked signature on credit card before accepting payment" and an example of "poor" work behaviour for a receptionist could be "did not give company name when answering the telephone".

One of the main strengths of this method is that it focuses on job behaviours, so performance rather than personality is judged. This makes this type of appraisal more job relevant, too. It is easier to give employees either positive or negative feedback based on specific examples of behaviour at work.

A disadvantage of the critical incident method is that it is time-consuming for the appraiser to have to write down these incidents on a daily or weekly basis. Good observation skills are required. Moreover, if different examples of good and poor behaviours are identified for each employee, comparison becomes a problem.

Critical incident may be useful in workplaces where it is important that certain procedures be followed, such as health and safety practices on a building site.

Checklist

A list of work behaviours relevant to the job is drawn up and the evaluator simply ticks those behaviours that apply to the employee.

Table 7.1: Sample of Checklist Items for Appraising a Sales Assistant

	Yes	No
Does the employee offer to help customers?	___	___
Is the employee courteous to customers?	___	___
Is the employee helpful to other employees?	___	___
Does the employee keep the shelves stocked?	___	___
Does the employee follow shop procedures when accepting payment?	___	___

One of the strengths of the checklist is that it is job related. In addition, it makes it easier to compare employees. Another advantage is that it is much simpler for the evaluator to tick behaviours than to write an essay-style report on each employee.

However, if there are a number of job categories in the organisation, a checklist has to be made out for each one and this can be time-consuming.

Like the critical incident method, the checklist can be useful when specific behaviours of the job can be identified as being essential.

Rating

This method requires the use of a scale on which certain behaviours or characteristics are listed. The appraiser decides to what degree the employee exhibits the behaviours or possesses the characteristics, for example from poor to excellent.

Table 7.2: **Sample of Rating Scale for Appraising a Sales Assistant**

Main duties	*1*	*2*	*3*	*4*	*5*	*Comment*
Assisting customers						
Co-operating with other employees						
Stocking shelves						
Dealing with complaints						
Dealing with suppliers						
Rating scale *1 Poor, 2 Satisfactory, 3 Good, 4 Very Good, 5 Excellent*						

Rating is a popular method of performance appraisal, probably because it is very convenient for the appraiser to use. In addition, it is easy to make comparisons among employees.

However, it can be difficult to measure personality or behavioural traits on a rating scale. Moreover, there is a danger with some rating scales that users might simply choose the middle value for all appraisees. This is called the *error of central tendency* and can be reduced by using certain rating scales, such as the forced choice technique, which do not have a middle value.

Ranking

Ranking means putting in order. A soldier's rank indicates their position in the army hierarchy in order of importance. In the workplace, employees can be ranked from best to worst. The individual ranking method requires the appraiser to list the employees in order from highest to lowest. The group order ranking method requires the evaluator to place employees into a particular classification such as "top quarter", "second quarter" and so on. The main advantages of this appraisal method are that it is easy to carry out and that it facilitates the comparison of employees.

However, with a small number of workers who are all very good, some will have to be placed in the "last quarter", which may give a misleading picture of these workers' performance. Another problem with ranking is that the degrees of difference are not specified. This means that there may only be a tiny difference between the first and second worker and then a bigger gap between the second and third. Ranking can be difficult to carry out where large numbers of employees are involved.

Paired Comparison

This method involves comparing each worker to every other worker. Two workers are compared at a time and a decision is made as to who is superior. Each employee is given a score, which depends on the number of times the individual is the preferred member. Finally, all employees are ranked. This is often seen as a more comprehensive and fair way of ranking employees but, of course, the weaknesses of ranking, as mentioned above, apply here, too.

Management by Objectives (MBO)

Another method of evaluating employee performance involves assessing the extent to which job objectives are achieved. Objectives are derived from the organisation's strategic plan and cascaded down to departments and individual employees. This process involves the manager and employee agreeing a number of objectives to be achieved by the employee for a particular period. The period will vary from organisation to organisation, with the usual timescale being twelve months. However, a certain amount of flexibility is necessary to allow for business fluctuations. During this time, a number of interim reviews take place between the manager and employee to determine how well the objectives are being achieved. It may be necessary to amend objectives if business circumstances have changed.

In order for objectives to be meaningful, it is important that they conform to certain criteria, for example SMART.

Specific   Objectives should be precisely defined and clearly understood by both parties.

Measurable   Where possible, objectives should include numerical targets.

Agreed   Managers should define and agree objectives with employees. In order to be motivating, objectives need to be "owned" by employees.

Realistic   Objectives should be challenging but achievable.

Time-related Put time limits on all objectives and set interim review dates.

Table 7.3: Example of Objectives for Sales Representative

Objective	Standard to be achieved	Review date	Completion date
To increase sales of Quincho soft drinks	by 5%	—/—/—	—/—/—
Respond to customer enquiries promptly	within 24 hrs of call	—/—/—	—/—/—

Other objectives may include:

• reduce number of accidents

• improve quality of product

• improve quality of service

• increase production

• reduce bad debts

• reduce customer complaints.

One of the main advantages of MBO is that assessment of performance is based on specific objectives. Moreover, employees have greater direction and control over their work, which can lead to greater motivation, and ultimately greater overall organisation performance. MBO also contributes towards improved interpersonal relationships between manager and employee due to the increase in communication.

The disadvantages sometimes associated with the MBO appraisal method are that the process may become bureaucratic and time-consuming for the manager. Furthermore, employees may only concentrate on those goals that will be rewarded and neglect other responsibilities.

Table 7.4: Summary of Appraisal Methods

Method	Strengths	Weaknesses
Essay	• easy to use • flexible	• no structure • difficult to compare employees • can be subjective • time-consuming to carry out
Critical incident	• focus on job behaviours	• time-consuming to construct • difficult to compare employees
Checklist	• easy to use • job related • easy comparison	• time-consuming to construct
Rating	• easy to use • easy comparison	• not suitable for all characteristics • error of central tendency • time-consuming to construct
Ranking	• easy to use • easy comparison	• degrees of difference not specified • difficult with large numbers
Paired comparison	• easy to use • more comprehensive approach than ranking	• as for ranking
Management by Objectives	• specific objectives set • motivates employees • improves communication	• time-consuming • can be bureaucratic • employees may neglect other duties

CONTRIBUTORS TO THE APPRAISAL PROCESS

Immediate Supervisor

Most appraisals are carried out by the employee's immediate supervisor or manager. They may not get to see every detail of how the employee carries out tasks, but they see the result of the employee's performance, such as whether sales targets were reached or deadlines were met.

Peer Assessment

Colleagues are often asked to evaluate each other's work performance. This is called peer assessment. Colleagues may be in a better position to judge work performance, as they see the actual behaviour of their co-workers on a day-to-day basis as they carry out tasks and interact with customers. Research has shown that this form of assessment can be reliable (Latham and Wexley, 1981). It is not commonly used, however, perhaps because employees feel uncomfortable about assessing other workers and because employees may react badly to peer appraisal and be more likely to accept the appraisal of a superior.

Customers

Customers are a useful source of appraisal information. This is done by analysing comment cards and customer complaints. "Secret shoppers" are used to assess the techniques used by sales staff, for instance.

Subordinates

Subordinates are a potential source of appraisal information, too. Information from subordinates may be limited in value, as they may not know much about the work done by their superior. However, it can be useful in evaluating management style. It is not frequently used, probably because workers feel uncomfortable about assessing a superior and managers may find it harder to accept these evaluations. It may interfere with the authority a manager has over subordinates.

Self-appraisal

Employees can evaluate themselves and are often asked to do so as part of the appraisal process and in preparation for the appraisal interview. All of the methods described above are open to bias and self-appraisal is no exception.

360-degree Appraisal

Multi-rater assessment, or 360-degree feedback, involves collecting information from all of the sources mentioned above. When external sources such as customers and suppliers are included, it is sometimes called 540-degree feedback. This type of appraisal provides information on different aspects of the employee's performance, giving a rounded view of the individual's strengths and weaknesses. However, it can be difficult to gather information from so many sources. In addition, this method is time-consuming and can be expensive.

THE APPRAISAL INTERVIEW

Most performance appraisals involve an appraisal interview as part of the process. The appraisal interview tends to follow one of three interviewing styles.

The tell-and-sell method begins when the appraisee is told the results of their appraisal. The manager then gets their acceptance of the evaluation and tells them how to improve. When this approach is used, the employee has little involvement in the appraisal process. It may be appropriate in situations where workers have very little experience and need direction.

The tell-and-listen approach also begins with the result of the appraisal being communicated to the employee. It differs from the tell-and-sell method in that the appraisee is encouraged to respond to the evaluation results.

The problem-solving style is completely different. The appraiser does not act as a judge, as in the previous two approaches. In fact the appraisal result is not communicated to the employee at this stage. Instead, the employee is encouraged to discuss any difficulties in their work situation and to consider the solutions. The final evaluation takes place as a result of the interview.

CONDUCTING THE APPRAISAL INTERVIEW

Careful planning prior to the appraisal interview is an essential element in successfully evaluating employee performance. Performance appraisal interviews tend to be conducted once or twice a year and should be a two-way communication process between manager and employee. The following advice is broadly based on the MBO approach, but can be adapted to suit specific organisational needs.

Before the Appraisal Interview

1. Give employees sufficient notice of the date and time of the appraisal interview and some indication of its duration. New employees should be given some background information on the appraisal interview process to ensure that they are able to participate as fully as possible.

2. Ask employees to review their own performance by completing a self-appraisal form. Alternatively, you could ask employees to write down a few points with regard to specific aspects of their performance that they consider they did well, areas where they can improve and to identify any factors that might have affected performance.

3. Review all evidence and relevant documentation relating to employee performance, ensuring that you make a note of any adverse circumstances that may have had a negative effect.

During the Appraisal Interview

1. The appraiser and appraisee should have highlighted and dealt with any difficulties as they arose during the review period. Consequently, there should be no surprises during the interview as good management practice advocates continuous review of performance and feedback to employees.

2. The interview should be conducted in a positive atmosphere, with the emphasis being placed, as far as possible, on the positive aspects of performance. However, where the employee has experienced some difficulties in achieving acceptable standards of performance, these should not be ignored, but discussed on the basis of providing opportunities for improvement. Coaching, counselling or training and development activities may be identified to help overcome difficulties.

3. Having reviewed past performance, attention should focus on agreeing future objectives, identifying training and development needs and drawing up action plans.

4. Always close the appraisal interview on a positive note, as this will ensure that the employee does not remember the experience in a negative light.

After the Appraisal Interview

1. Write up interview notes, together with objectives and training needs, and pass to employee for agreement and signature.

2. Prepare action plans for job objectives and training requirements agreed during appraisal interview.

3. Remember that performance appraisal interviews are confidential.

(See Appendix 5 for a sample performance-appraisal form.)

Chapter 8

MOTIVATION: GETTING THE MOST OUT OF YOUR EMPLOYEES

"There is a correlation between organisations that go to a lot of trouble to motivate their staff and profitable business performance."

(Pettinger, 1994)

This chapter will help you to:

- discover why knowledge of motivation is essential for effective management
- identify workers' needs and consider how they can be met by the organisation
- recognise the importance of the work environment in relation to employee motivation
- consider how job design can affect levels of motivation
- be aware of how workers' motivation can be affected if they feel unfairly treated
- consider the role of goal setting in motivating employees
- examine how to retain good employees.

MOTIVATION AND HRM

For many managers, the concept of motivation is an abstract one. You may instinctively know whether an employee is motivated or not, but you may find it difficult to isolate the cause or to find a solution. Theories of work motivation attempt to understand why people behave the way they do at work; they try to explain why some people work very hard, for example, or why some employees try to get away with doing as little as possible. Managers and supervisors can use this information to try to improve levels of motivation in workers.

You may remember from Chapter 1 that the human resource style of management views employees as a valuable resource. "Soft" HRM recognises individual differences among employees and concentrates on nurturing and developing staff as a means of achieving organisational aims. A knowledge and understanding of human motivation is essential for managing employees effectively. It will help you to deal with problems such as absenteeism, employee turnover, low morale and low quality or productivity. The concepts of employee motivation can be usefully applied in strategies for effective reward management (see Chapter 9).

Some motivation theories try to pinpoint *what* motivates people. Things that can motivate people include money, job security, prestige and the need for achievement. Other theories focus on *how* the process of motivation takes place by trying to understand how workers think. Drawing information from a number of theories, this chapter offers some advice for managers dealing with problems of motivation in the workplace.

To help you to understand the factors that influence motivation, consider the following questions:

* What incentives can you offer to employees in return for high performance?

* Do your employees have an opportunity to reach their full potential?

* Do your employees value the rewards on offer?

* Is the work environment conducive to motivating employees?

* Are jobs designed in such a way as to maximise motivation?

* Do your employees feel they are fairly treated compared to their colleagues and to workers in other organisations?

* Do your employees have targets to achieve? Do your employees feel that these targets are attainable? Are they challenging enough?

EXPLORING MOTIVATION IN ORGANISATIONS

Assess Employees' Needs

Some theorists believe that identifying workers' needs is the key to motivation. If a manager knows what an employee needs, relevant incentives can be offered in return for hard work, reduced absenteeism and so on. You can identify employee needs at various stages of the employment relationship. For example, both the selection and appraisal interviews can be used to find out what motivates employees. You can also collect this information during everyday interactions with your staff.

It is important to remember, too, that people's needs can change over time.

Maslow's (1943) "hierarchy of needs" is a popular theory of motivation. It describes five levels of need that an individual may have and assumes that workers will be motivated to work their way up through the levels in order to satisfy their needs and reach their fullest potential. A manager has to identify towards which level of needs each employee is working.

Physiological or Basic Needs

The most basic level in Maslow's hierarchy represents physiological needs. These are the things we need to survive and include food, water, air, sunlight and rest. You can cater for these basic needs by providing:

- an adequate wage or salary
- canteen facilities
- drinking water
- ventilation
- air conditioning (and heat)
- rest breaks
- toilet facilities.

In fact, organisations have a legal responsibility to provide their employees with most of the above. For example, the Safety, Health and Welfare at Work (Miscellaneous Welfare Provisions) Regulations, 1995 outlines the employer's duty to provide drinking water and facilities for taking meals. The National Minimum Wage Act, 2000 provides for basic pay and the Organisation of Working Time Act, 1997 specifies the legislation regarding rest breaks. See Chapter 13 for more information on employment legislation.

Security Needs

According to Maslow's theory, once an individual's physiological needs have been taken care of, they become less important and the individual now focuses on security needs. You can consider the following ways to help workers feel secure in their job and safe in their work environment:

- provide contracts and permanent positions
- organise pension plans

• offer health insurance

• ensure a safe work environment by adhering to health and safety regulations

• prepare and implement policies on bullying and sexual harassment.

Employers are legally obliged to provide a safe and secure work environment for employees. See the Terms of Employment (Information) Act, 1994 and 2001, the Safety, Health and Welfare at Work Act, 1989 and the Pensions (Amendment) Act, 2002.

Due to the changing and often uncertain business environment that most organisations operate in, it is not always possible to provide permanent contracts to employees. You may have to explain to staff that you can offer a short-term contract but cannot guarantee a long-term one at this point. You can point out some of the advantages that your employees enjoy, such as challenging work, flexible working hours and so on. See Chapter 11 for advice on how to communicate with employees.

Belongingness Needs

The next level of needs is belongingness. Everybody, to some extent, has the need for friendship, to be liked by colleagues and to fit in at work. Here are some ways that you can help employees to satisfy this need:

• provide an induction programme (see Chapter 6)

• encourage teamwork

• organise office parties

• set up a social club

• establish a mentoring system.

While Maslow felt that workers would be motivated to satisfy their basic needs, another theorist, Herzberg (1966) disagreed. Herzberg felt that workers would be very dissatisfied if they did not have enough of these basic things but that they would not actually be motivated by pay, security and other lower order needs. Therefore, according to Herzberg, providing for a worker's basic needs can prevent dissatisfaction and unrest at work but will not lead to motivation. Herzberg believed that workers are motivated to achieve higher order needs, such as the top two levels of Maslow's hierarchy.

Help Employees to Reach their Fullest Potential

Humanistic psychologists believe that we all have an innate desire to be the best that we can be. They believe that we become unhappy and frustrated if we are prevented from reaching our fullest potential. McGregor's (1960) Theory Y suggests that people are ambitious, enjoy work and want responsibility. However, an employee's attitude to work is affected by how they are perceived and treated by colleagues and management.

Esteem Needs

The fourth level in Maslow's hierarchy is esteem. This refers to workers' needs for confidence, recognition and respect in their jobs. There are a number of ways that you can try to fulfil the esteem needs of your employees. These include:

- "employee of the month" awards
- promotion
- job title
- giving the employee more responsibility
- placing value on the individual's advice or suggestions.

Self-Actualisation

Self-actualisation is the final level in Maslow's hierarchy of needs. You can help your employees to reach their fullest potential by:

- providing opportunities for promotion
- encouraging creativity
- setting challenging work assignments.

According to Maslow, though, a particular level of needs does not motivate individuals until the ones before it have been satisfied. If this is the case, an employee will not be motivated to earn more respect and prestige at work if the basic needs have not been met.

Alderfer (1972), on the other hand, believed that while an individual could get enough of the lower level needs and not want to get any more of those basic things, higher level needs are never satisfied. This implies that an employee can always be motivated to satisfy esteem and self-actualisation needs. If this is true, it is essential for a manager to recognise the importance of higher order needs.

Figure 8.1: Maslow's Hierarchy of Needs

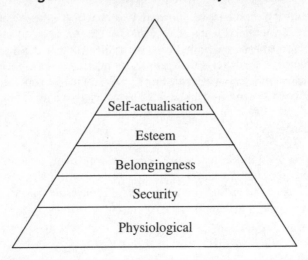

Choose Rewards that Employees Value

You cannot assume that every worker will be motivated by the same incentives. A lot depends on how much value an employee places on certain things. Expectancy theory predicts that workers are motivated by pay and other rewards only if the employee values these rewards. This theory suggests that rather than identifying the level of needs a worker is focusing on, you should try to identify what the employee values. This could be money, free time or more responsibility.

Alderfer (1972) thought that a person could be motivated by more than one need at any particular time. For example, a worker may try to satisfy a basic need, such as earning enough money to survive, and at the same time focus on a higher level need, such as recognition for work done. The organisation should facilitate good performance by providing adequate opportunities for employees to satisfy their varying needs.

Provide a Suitable Work Environment

McClelland (1961) is another theorist who believed that an individual could be trying to satisfy a number of needs at the same time. He studied the need for achievement, the need for affiliation and the need for autonomy. To apply McClelland's ideas you need to understand your employees' needs and provide an appropriate work environment. In this way, you can help your employees to perform to the best of their abilities.

Need for Achievement

People with a high need for achievement work best in challenging environments. They thrive when they have a goal to achieve but become bored and demotivated when they are not being challenged. People with a high need for achievement often make good salespeople and do well in jobs where they have targets to reach. You need to ensure that a challenging work environment exists for these individuals. Employees in this category should be provided with regular feedback on their work performance. They need to know how they are making progress in relation to their goals.

Need for Affiliation

Employees with a high need for affiliation (or belongingness) have a strong need for approval and reassurance from others. They tend to choose jobs high in interpersonal contact and work best in a supportive, co-operative work environment where teamwork is highly valued. Employees with a high need for affiliation do not work well if these needs are not met within the workplace. You need to ensure that these employees have the support they need in order to perform at their best.

Need for Autonomy

Employees with a high need for autonomy find it hard to work when there are too many rules and regulations. They often prefer to work alone and like to control the pace of their work, as in the case of specialised tradespeople. These workers are at their best when they are given some leeway to decide exactly how to complete a job. They are most suited to work that requires creative flair or problem solving, such as design work and research. Highly structured work environments may not be conducive to improving levels of motivation for these workers.

You can use McClelland's work to get the best performance from workers either by employing people most suited to the existing work environment or by providing an appropriate work environment for existing employees.

Look at how Jobs are Designed

Job design is how organisations define and structure jobs. Several writers have tackled the area of job design (see Armstrong, 2001) and suggest characteristics which have an important effect on employee motivation.

Ideally, jobs should be designed in such a way that employees:

- are responsible for a complete piece of work, or at least a significant part of it, so that they can recognise a whole product as the result of their work
- have the opportunity to use a variety of skills
- feel that their work is important
- are responsible for setting goals and deciding how their work will be carried out
- monitor their own performance and progress
- receive constructive feedback on their performance.

It is also worth considering flexible working arrangements such as flexi-time, job-sharing, part-time contracts, home working and sabbaticals. Flexibility on your part may result in employees being flexible and adaptable in return and will reduce costs such as rent, power and telephone.

Ensure that Employees Feel Fairly Treated

Adams' (1963) equity theory of motivation contends that motivation at work is influenced by *perceived* fairness in the workplace. Employees assess what they bring to their jobs and what they get in return and they compare this to what other workers put in and get back. Examples of what people bring to their jobs include experience, qualifications, effort and time; pay, experience, contacts and recognition are some of the things they get in return.

If workers feel unfairly treated in comparison to co-workers or to people with similar jobs in other organisations, they will be motivated to restore equity in the situation. Asking for a pay rise, making less effort and leaving the job are common reactions to perceived inequity in the workplace.

As a manager, you have to be aware that this type of comparison exists and that there are potentially negative consequences for the organisation if workers feel unfairly treated. What you believe to be fair is irrelevant if employees perceive the situation to be inequitable. Employees behave in reaction to their own perception of the situation, not that of the manager. It is important that you ensure that employees feel equitably treated.

Set Goals

Setting targets is another way to try to motivate employees. Earlier in the chapter, it was noted that people with a high need for achievement work best in a challenging work environment. Humanistic psychologists such as Maslow and Rogers believe that all people have a natural desire to reach their fullest potential and be the best that they can be.

These theorists believe that goal setting is healthy both for the worker and for the organisation. A manager needs to be concerned about how high these targets are set. On the one hand, if the targets are set too low, some workers may not feel challenged enough and will not make much effort. On the other hand, it is not advisable to set targets too high either: expectancy theory predicts that an individual will not be motivated if they cannot see a link between their effort and achievement of the target. In other words, if a worker feels that the goal is impossible to reach, no matter how much effort is made, motivation will be reduced. Targets need to be achievable. It is best if targets can be agreed by management and employees. See the section on Management by Objectives in Chapter 7.

STAFF RETENTION

Davies (2001) points out the costs to the organisation if a valued employee leaves. Firstly, there is the time and expense involved in finding a replacement. Then there is the potential damage to your organisation's public image if a high-profile employee departs or if it becomes widely perceived that you have difficulty holding on to staff. In addition, since many of those who leave will go to rivals, taking with them knowledge and contacts, your competitive position may be threatened.

Here is some advice for retaining employees:

* Provide a comprehensive induction programme for new employees, as people are most likely to leave their jobs in the early days. See Chapter 6 for more information on induction.

* Ensure that the reward package is perceived as fair by employees, taking into account their qualifications and experience and in comparison to what other organisations are offering for the same job. See Chapter 9 for more information on reward management.

* Facilitate employees to develop a sense of commitment by encouraging a sense of belonging and value to the organisation. See previous discussion on motivating employees.

* Ensure that employees are given the opportunity to make suggestions and air their grievances. See Chapter 11 on communicating with employees and Chapter 12 on dispute resolution.

- Where possible, be flexible with employees, both in terms of job design and employee lifestyle. Consider flexitime, job-sharing, part-time contracts, home working and sabbaticals.

Chapter 9

REWARD MANAGEMENT: MANAGING THE REWARD PACKAGE

> "Managing rewards involves the establishment and maintenance of adequate remuneration systems which attract, retain and motivate the organisation's workforce in line with business objectives."
>
> (Gunnigle and Flood, 1990: 114)

This chapter will help you to:

- understand the importance of reward management
- identify the factors that influence pay levels
- consider the different methods of job evaluation
- examine the essential characteristics of a reward package.

THE IMPORTANCE OF REWARD MANAGEMENT

The decisions you make regarding pay and benefits play a role in achieving HRM outcomes and objectives by:

- attracting potential employees
- retaining good employees
- motivating employees.

Reward management, therefore, is linked to other aspects of the HR role in an organisation such as planning, recruitment, training and motivation. The resulting HR strategies should complement organisational objectives such as gaining competitive advantage and increasing levels of job satisfaction.

FACTORS THAT INFLUENCE PAY LEVELS

The main factors influencing pay levels are:

- the economic climate
- the labour market
- legislation
- trade union and employee demands.

The Economic Climate

In times of economic prosperity, workers and trade unions often put pressure on employers to increase their pay. In fact, the number of industrial disputes and strikes increases when the economy is doing well. This is because organisations are making more money and employees want to make sure they get some of it. There is little point in pushing for a pay rise during an economic recession when there is no money available. Another economic factor is inflation. When inflation levels are high, prices go up and workers look for pay increases to match the cost of living.

Inflation and economic prosperity influence what an organisation can afford to pay. This is probably one of the first factors that the organisation should consider before making an offer to employees. Moreover, economic factors influence what other organisations can pay. In an effort to recruit the best employees, an organisation might choose to pay a little more than the going rate.

The Labour Market

The availability of workers in the labour market influences pay levels. If an organisation is having difficulty recruiting workers in general, or workers with specific skills or qualifications, they may have to offer a better reward package to attract people. In the last few years, people with specialised IT skills could command large salaries and fringe benefits. However, if the supply of workers or skills is greater than the demand for them, the organisation is in a position to be less generous. For this reason, unskilled workers have less bargaining power when it comes to decisions on pay.

Legislation

Two main pieces of legislation affect reward systems in Irish organisations:

1. The National Minimum Wage Act, 2000, with some exceptions, means that employees are guaranteed at least €6.35/hour from 1 October 2002. This figure will increase to €7/hour from February 2004.

2. The Employment Equality Act, 1998 states that employees must be paid the same for like work and cannot be discriminated against on the basis of sex, age, disability, marital status, family status, sexual orientation, race, religion or membership of a travelling community.

Employment legislation is covered in more detail in Chapter 13.

Trade Union and Employee Demands

When the economy is doing well and there is low unemployment, workers, often represented by trade unions, are in a relatively powerful position. The demands of individual workers or collective bargaining by unions can result in pay increases. In fact, there have been times when unions were so successful in negotiating pay deals that they were accused of causing increases in inflation.

JOB EVALUATION

Armstrong (2001: 631) defines job evaluation as "a systematic process for establishing the relative worth of jobs within an organisation". If you are deciding how much to pay an employee, you first need to assess the value of the job to the organisation. This section describes the main methods of evaluating jobs. Some of these can be used quite easily while others will require professional expertise.

Job Ranking

Ranking means "placing in a hierarchy". To use this method, you need to list all of the jobs in your organisation. Then rank them in order of importance or value to the organisation. Just think about the job as a whole. You do not need to consider elements such as qualifications required or amount of responsibility involved. Once you have ranked the jobs, you then arrange them into groups or grades. Finally, you decide on the pay levels for each grade. Jobs within a particular grade will merit the same pay.

Job ranking is a straightforward way of evaluating jobs. It is easy to understand and quick and inexpensive to operate. This method is probably most useful in organisations with a small number of jobs.

One of the weaknesses of job ranking is that it is subjective. This means that it is possible that different people will rank jobs in different orders. Since standards for ranking are not defined, it may be difficult to justify why jobs are put in a particular order. Another limitation is that this method of job evaluation is not analytical. In other words, the job is considered as a whole and factors such as skills, responsibility and working conditions are not taken into account. This makes it difficult to justify pay differences following job evaluation. Finally, ranking is difficult where large numbers of jobs are involved.

Paired Comparison

This method of job evaluation is a more systematic version of ranking. Compile a list of jobs and then compare each job to every other job. Give two points to whichever of the two jobs you decide is more valuable. If you decide that the jobs are of equal value, give one point each. The job that is worth less gets no points. When each job has been compared to every other job, add up all the points. Now rank the jobs in order from the most points to the least.

Paired comparison is a more systematic and comprehensive approach to job evaluation than simple job ranking. Apart from this, both methods share similar advantages and disadvantages.

Job Classification

Job classification is similar to job ranking but uses a different approach. If you want to use the job classification system, you first decide how many pay grades you want, for example grades one to five. You base your grading structure on differences in skill, qualifications, responsibility and so on. Then you place the jobs into these grades. As with job ranking, the jobs are not broken down into components but are assessed as a whole.

This method of job evaluation is easy to operate. By first deciding on a grading structure, some standards for ranking are defined and it will be easy to fit new jobs into the classification structure once it has been established. Job classification is suitable for dealing with large numbers of employees.

However, job classification becomes complicated when there is a wide range of jobs to evaluate. Some jobs may not fit neatly into just one grade.

Points Rating

This commonly used method of job evaluation involves breaking down each job into a number of job factors. Benge (1944) suggested the following:

- skill requirements

- responsibility

- physical requirements

- mental requirements

- working conditions.

You allocate points for each element of the job and add them up.

The points rating method of job evaluation is more objective than job ranking or job classification. It is also analytical, which means that the job is broken down into components for evaluation purposes. Because standards of comparison are clearly defined, it is easier to explain differences in pay following job evaluation.

A disadvantage of the points rating method is that it is more complex than ranking or job classification. It is also more time-consuming and costly to develop. Moreover, even though this method of job evaluation is more objective than the others discussed so far in this chapter, it still relies on subjective judgement to some extent.

The Hay Method

The Hay Method is widely used and is traditionally associated with evaluating managerial and professional jobs.

This method relies on three main factors:

- Know-how

- Problem solving

- Accountability

Each of these factors is further subdivided and allocated points based on comparisons made among jobs.

The Hay Method is more objective than many other approaches, which contributes to its wide acceptance. The main drawback lies in its complexity. In addition, this method of job evaluation is time-consuming and expensive to develop. A certain amount of subjective judgement is required.

Competence-based Job Evaluation

With this type of job evaluation, you focus on the *person* who performs
the job and their competence and abilities rather than on the job title or
grade. The following are considered important:

- interpersonal skills
- communication skills
- technical knowledge
- decision-making ability
- team working and leadership skills.

The key strength of competence-based or skill-based job evaluation is
that it focuses on the person rather than on the job. However, a criticism
of this method is that there may be too much emphasis on the individual's skills and knowledge and not enough on how productive the job is.
Another drawback is the complexity of the approach.

THE REWARD PACKAGE

Reward management involves making decisions about the amount and
the form of payment employees should receive.
   The main elements of a reward package are:

- pay, which refers to the basic wage or salary
- incentives, which are rewards for performance beyond normal
  expectations
- benefits, also known as indirect pay, which include pensions and health
  insurance.

Pay, incentives and benefits combine in a number of ways to form
different types of payment systems.

Payment Systems

The *flat-rate system* is the traditional approach to payment: people are
paid according to the time they spend at work. Pay can be calculated on
an hourly, weekly or annual basis. This system provides stable earnings
for employees and the payroll is easy to organise. It is also useful when
performance criteria are difficult to establish. A potential problem is
that if everyone is paid the same then there is no incentive for employees
to work harder.

An *incremental pay scale* is a form of the flat-rate system where employees are paid for the time they spend at work but are guaranteed an extra amount or increment every year. This system is designed to encourage employees to stay with the same organisation for a long period. Incremental pay schemes are generally accepted as fair, as they tend to be based on length of service. It usually takes a few years to work your way up the scale, which might be frustrating for ambitious workers, and once you reach the top of the scale there is little incentive to work hard any more. This payment system is common in large bureaucratic organisations.

Incentive pay systems involve making a payment in addition to the flat rate based on performance. This extra payment can be based on an individual employee's performance or on the performance of a group, such as a sales team. While this approach can be good for motivation and is useful when it is difficult to measure individual performance, it can cause harmful competition within the organisation. Examples include bonuses and commission.

Individual payment by results is a system where the amount that a person is paid depends on the amount they produce. The employee is not paid for the time it took to complete the job but instead for its completion. Also known as piecework, this approach is best used in work environments, such as factories, where it is easy to measure the quantity of work completed. This pay system provides an incentive to increase effort and decrease the amount of time taken to do the job. However, it makes organising the payroll more complicated and there is a danger that quality may suffer. It is often seen as an unacceptable system as there is no guarantee of a minimum income.

Performance-related pay, also known as merit rating, is used as an incentive in situations where the actual work rate is difficult to measure. Assessing employees' performance fairly is difficult to do and this is the main reason that trade unions tend to oppose performance-related pay. In order for this approach to be effective, it is important that employees are involved in setting up the system and that performance criteria are clearly defined.

Gain sharing is an approach to reward management that involves rewarding employees for the organisation's success. It can take the form of profit sharing, where employees are promised a bonus when the organisation makes a profit. Another example is share ownership, where employees are given shares in the company. This form of payment system is used to encourage co-operation between management and workers and increase commitment to the organisation. The problem is that employees may find it difficult to see a link between their own individual performance and that of the organisation.

Competence or skill-based payment systems focus on the worker's level of skill rather than on the job itself. There is a basic rate of pay for having the minimum level of skill and employees will be paid more if they have or acquire new skills that assist them in their jobs. This approach encourages employees to update their skills and qualifications continuously.

Another element of the rewards package incorporates non-monetary rewards. These benefits include extra holiday time, health insurance, sick pay and pensions – none of which an employer is obliged to provide.

ESSENTIAL CHARACTERISTICS OF A REWARD SYSTEM

Lawler (1977) outlined five "essential characteristics" of an effective reward system. These elements should be considered when putting a reward package together.

Reward Level

Employees' needs were discussed in Chapter 8. You must ensure that the reward level you offer is enough to live on as well as satisfy your employees' other basic needs, such as security and esteem. Because the cost of living is higher in Dublin, for example, employers often have to offer higher basic salaries than are paid for similar jobs in other parts of the country. The minimum reward level has been determined by legislation (National Minimum Wage Act, 2000).

Individuality

Your reward system should be able to provide for the individuality of employees and be flexible enough to meet their different needs. The concept of valence was discussed in Chapter 8, recognising that different employees value different things. Some organisations offer a choice of fringe benefits so that employees can choose, for example, between a pension contribution and extra holiday time. This is known as the "cafeteria approach": a flexible pay system that allows employees to choose their own reward or combination of rewards. The concept of individuality is also linked to performance-related pay. You have to make decisions as to whether all employees will receive the same rewards or whether rewards should depend on effort or results.

Internal Equity

Remember that workers compare themselves to other workers in the organisation. This is the main point of Adam's equity theory (Chapter 8). Employees want to feel fairly treated when they consider what they put into their jobs and what they get in return. It is essential that workers perceive internal equity in the pay system devised by the organisation. A transparent reward system with clearly explained differentials is necessary.

External Equity

Employees also compare themselves to workers in other similar organisations. Again, they want to feel fairly treated in comparison with what is being offered elsewhere. It is important when you design your pay system that you find out as much as you can about what competing organisations are offering. One of the reasons for a shortage of nurses in Ireland at the moment is that many nurses are choosing to work in the pharmaceutical industry, which offers better working conditions and more money. If you want to retain valued members of staff and attract highly qualified and experienced employees, you will have to ensure that the reward you offer compares favourably with that offered by your competitors.

Trust

The final characteristic described by Lawler is trust. Employees need to believe that rewards will be given for work done and targets achieved. In addition, management must trust that employees will work to the level expected of them in order to get these rewards.

Chapter 10

CHANGE MANAGEMENT: MANAGING CHANGE EFFECTIVELY

"Planning, implementing and coping with change has been, and seems likely to remain, one of the main challenges facing managers…"

(Carnall, 1990: 2)

This chapter will help you to:

- understand the importance of managing change effectively
- identify factors that may force you to introduce change
- examine why employees may resist change
- manage employee resistance to change
- plan a change programme.

THE IMPORTANCE OF MANAGING CHANGE EFFECTIVELY

In order to compete and grow within a challenging economy, all organisations need to introduce changes from time to time. Many of these changes will emerge from your organisation's planning process and be consistent with your business plan: for example, you may decide to enter new markets or expand into new geographical areas. By adopting a proactive approach to managing change, you will be able to control the rate and pace of change and implement it in a planned manner. However, the dynamic nature of business means that it is not always possible to predict and plan for change and you may occasionally have to react quickly to circumstances outside your control.

The manner in which you manage change will greatly influence your employees' acceptance of the change initiative. For some employees the proposed change may represent excitement and an opportunity to acquire new skills; for other employees, the proposed change may represent a threat to their existing role and result in resistance to the change initiative.

FORCES OF CHANGE

Forces of change can be viewed from two perspectives: those external to the organisation and those that emerge from within the organisation.

Examples of External Forces of Change

* Changes in employment law
* Demand for product or service
* Competition
* Health and safety
* Taxation, interest and exchange rates
* Inflation
* Changes in lifestyle
* Availability of labour
* Transport and infrastructure
* Technology and telecommunications

Examples of Internal Forces of Change

* Cost control
* Levels of productivity
* Conflict
* Absenteeism/staff turnover
* Organisational goals
* Management style

Resistance to Change

When considering the introduction of any new change initiative within the workplace, you should try to anticipate if there is likely to be any resistance. Resistance to change can come from both individuals and groups of employees who have a vested interest in maintaining the status quo, for example members of trade unions or specialist employees, such as technicians.

Specifically, employees may resist change for the following reasons:

- fear of losing their status within the organisation, which may be associated with change in title, loss of own office or reduction in number of employees reporting to them
- changes to wages or bonus payments may make it difficult for employees to meet existing financial commitments
- disruption to existing working relationships that may have been developed over a long period
- threat to existing expertise and doubts about their ability to acquire new skills
- possible increase in workload and responsibility
- doubts about the need for and feasibility of proposed change
- resentment due to lack of involvement in the change process
- fear of losing their job and not being able to obtain suitable alternative employment
- misunderstanding the change and its implications
- lack of trust between employees and management.

Resistance to change may encourage management to re-examine their proposals. It may also encourage further discussion and lead to a better understanding of the need for change.

MANAGING RESISTANCE TO CHANGE

A key challenge for organisations is to manage resistance to change. Kotter and Schlesinger (1979) suggest that resistance to change can be managed by adopting one or more of the following approaches:

Communication and Education

Informing employees about the proposed change will help them to see the need for and logic of change. It will give you an opportunity to address any concerns that employees may have. This method of dealing with resistance to change is useful if resistance is based on inadequate or inaccurate information. However, this type of approach will take time and effort and requires that there is a good relationship between you and your employees; otherwise, employees may not trust what they hear.

Participation and Involvement

It might be a good idea to involve employees in the change process, especially those who are likely to resist the proposed change. Employees who have had a say are more likely to be committed to and support the change. If employees are not consulted, there is a risk that they will be uncooperative. This approach is time-consuming, so it may not be appropriate if change is required quickly.

Facilitation and Support

Employees may experience fear and anxiety during a period of change. Providing training, offering time off work following a demanding period or simply listening to your employees are all methods of providing facilitation and support. This method can be time-consuming and expensive.

Negotiation and Agreement

It may be possible for you to reduce resistance to change by offering incentives to resistors or their representatives. This method is useful when it is clear that someone is going to lose out as a result of the change. You might consider offering an increase in wages or salary for a change in work practice, a one-off payment or an extra day(s) of holidays. This can be an easy way to avoid major resistance but may prove to be expensive.

Manipulation and Co-optation

Sometimes you may have to manipulate events and selectively use information to reduce resistance. You could co-opt an influential employee onto your change team and give them a minor role in the change process. This is a relatively inexpensive method of gaining the support of employees but there is the risk that the co-opted employee may use their influence in ways that are not in the best interests of your organisation. Furthermore, the co-opted employee may feel deceived and this may create even more resistance.

Coercion

As a last resort, you may have to force employees to accept change. There is a risk involved here, as people resent being threatened and your employees may decide to take industrial action. This method is useful when speed is essential and when the change will not be popular no matter how it is introduced.

How to Plan for Change

Making changes in your organisation may be achieved by changing:

- the people (through selection and training)
- the way people work (for example by introducing teamwork)
- the way jobs are designed
- your technology.

The following steps provide guidelines on how to plan for change.

1. Identify the need for change in your organisation.

2. Think about what you will need in order to implement the change. This may include money, equipment, space, time and expertise.

3. Consider why employees might oppose your ideas and decide how to deal with this resistance. For suggestions, see the previous section on managing resistance to change.

4. Implement the change process. Set objectives and prepare an action plan.

5. Conduct regular reviews of the change process and make adjustments where necessary.

Part IV

EMPLOYMENT RELATIONS

Chapter 11

COMMUNICATION: COMMUNICATING WITH EMPLOYEES EFFECTIVELY

"Communication is fundamental to all working relationships; inept or inadequate communication causes more
controversy in business and industry than any other single
factor."

(Woolcott and Unwin, 1983: 1)

This chapter will help you to:

- understand the importance of effective communication within
  organisations
- distinguish between formal and informal communication
- know how the communication process works
- identify barriers to communication
- utilise different media of communication.

THE IMPORTANCE OF COMMUNICATION WITHIN ORGANISATIONS

The importance of effective communication when managing people cannot be underestimated; it has the potential to influence the profitability
of an organisation. For an organisation to be successful, it is essential
that it have a committed and motivated workforce. Much of this commitment and motivation is generated by communicating effectively with
employees. For example, effective communication is influential in motivating employees (see Chapter 8) by involving them in job design and
by bringing about change in the organisation by communicating with
them on the reasons for change (see Chapter 10).

Ineffective communication can lead to:

- suspicion and distrust between employees and management
- rumours and gossip
- inefficiency
- dissatisfied customers.

Listening to employees and affording them the opportunity to communicate with management and each other in a constructive manner can do
much to create a motivated and committed workforce.

FORMAL AND INFORMAL COMMUNICATION WITHIN BUSINESS

Communication in organisations can be either formal or informal. *Formal
communication* originates from management. Examples include policy
statements on health and safety, procedures for dealing with grievance
and disciplinary matters, job descriptions and person specifications.
Informal communication relates to owners and managers adopting a more
personal approach when communicating with their employees on a day-
to-day basis; this may be to deal with an immediate challenge, such as
locating a customer order or discussing the best way to solve a problem.
Informal communication is quick, accurate and can maintain good
working relationships amongst employees by encouraging them to deal
with issues as they arise.

Managers also need to be aware of the "grapevine", which can be
used by employees to communicate quickly outside the formal communication processes on any number of issues. Unfortunately, the "grapevine" is not always accurate, as it can lead to distortion of information
and can be the source of false rumours. However, that is not to say that
managers cannot use the "grapevine" for their own ends: for example, if
you want to "test the water" with regard to a proposed change in work
practice, you can "leak" the information informally and gauge the response.

COMMUNICATION PROCESS

To help understand the importance of effective communication within
business, it is worth taking some time to think about what happens when
you communicate.

As you can see in Figure 11.1, communication is a two-way process
between the person sending the message and the person(s) receiving the
message. It consists of six stages:

1. You decide to send a message (for example to arrange a meeting or
   request information).

2. Think about how best to get this message across – options include
   using words, diagrams, pictures and tables.

3. Now choose the most appropriate medium for the message, for

Figure 11.1: Communication Process

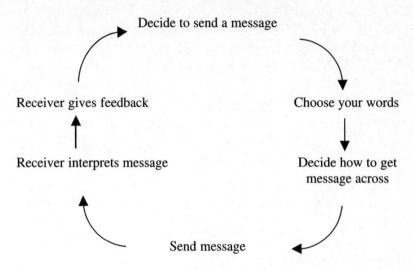

Decide to send a message

Receiver gives feedback

Choose your words

Receiver interprets message

Decide how to get message across

Send message

example report, letter, memo, meeting, e-mail, telephone, text.

4. Send your message – think about time and place.

5. Your message is received and interpreted by the receiver.

6. The receiver may reply or seek further clarification.

If further clarification is required, then the process has broken down and you have to start all over again

BARRIERS TO COMMUNICATION

Barriers to communication refer to any "blockage" that prevents a message being received and understood.

Structure of Message

Sometimes messages do not have a beginning, middle and end. If you are requesting a piece of information, it is important to be specific about:

• exactly what information you need

• the reason you need the information

• when you want to receive the information.

Language

The language used in any message should be appropriate for the message and for the people receiving the message. If you are presenting technical information to non-technical people, you need to choose language that they understand.

Information Overload

If too much information is given, the main message may be lost.

Timing

The timing of any message will influence how the message will be interpreted. If you want an employee to do some overtime, it would not be appropriate to ask them while they were dealing with a customer.

Background Noise

Background noise such as telephones, people coughing, talking or building work being carried out will hinder the ability of people to receive and interpret messages.

Inability to Listen

Listening is a key skill when managing people – you need to concentrate on what is being said.

Long Chain of Command

If your message has to pass through several people or layers of management, there is a danger that it will become distorted by the time it arrives at its destination.

MEDIA OF COMMUNICATION WITHIN ORGANISATIONS

Employees require a variety of information on a wide range of subjects to do their job more effectively. Organisations can avail of a number of communication media to help them manage their employees more effectively.

E-mail

Many organisations use e-mail to communicate, as it allows you to send a message quickly to a large number of people and receive a prompt reply. Scott (2000: 284) provides five guidelines for e-mail messages:

1. the rules for spelling, capitalisation, grammar and punctuation are the same as for any other form of writing

2. use the "subject heading" to make the main point of your message early

3. read the e-mail carefully before sending it

4. make sure that you only send the message to those who need to receive it

5. make sure your recipient can decode your attachments, graphics and any other accompaniments to your e-mail message.

E-mails are not suitable for sending personal or sensitive information and, of course, should your computer system crash, you run the risk of losing potentially important data.

Memoranda

Memoranda, commonly referred to as "memos", are short notes that are used by organisations for internal communication. The tone and style adopted in memos are usually less formal than in letters. Some organisations will use pre-printed forms for their memos; however, many computer packages now have memo templates that are easy to use and print.

As with e-mail, memos can be sent to one person or a number of people and generally deal with one subject or topic only. They can be used to remind people of a certain instruction, to invite people to a meeting or to give information on a new product or service.

There are a number of drawbacks when using memos:

- memos are not appropriate for urgent messages

- you have no way of knowing if your memo was received

- there may be a delay in receiving a response.

Notice Boards

A notice board is a useful method of communicating with all employees on a broad range of general business items, such as giving up-to-date data on business targets, reminding employees of a forthcoming training session or reinforcing company policy such as health and safety in the workplace. The posters or notices should be of sufficient size, well presented to attract attention and, most importantly, they should be relevant to the subject matter.

There are, however, a number of problems associated with the notice board. If the notice board is not located in a highly visible place, then staff may miss information. Notice boards are not suitable for displaying urgent or sensitive information. Finally, if notice boards are untidy, then they will be ignored.

Meetings

Organisations may need to call meetings to inform employees of organisational development issues or consult with employees on some aspect of organisational change. As meetings can take up much valuable time, it is important that they are structured and managed effectively. The following points can assist you in getting the most out of your meetings:

1. Establish the aim of your meeting. What do you hope to achieve? It is essential that your meeting has a purpose and that those attending the meeting are aware of what it is.

2. It is wise to have an agenda, a list of topics to be covered at the meeting, so that everyone is focused on the same outcome. Depending on the nature of the meeting, you can draw up the agenda yourself or you can ask those attending for suggestions. A useful tip is to place important items at the beginning of the meeting to be dealt with when people are more alert. The agenda should be sent out in plenty of time to allow people to prepare for the meeting.

3. One of the criticisms put forward by people attending meetings is that meetings go on for too long. As part of your meeting preparation, put a time limit on the duration of the meeting or, alternatively, put a time limit on agenda topics.

4. Only those people who are relevant to the meeting and prepared to make a meaningful contribution to the meeting should attend.

5. The chairperson of the meeting should control the meeting by encouraging participation by all members and not allowing the meeting to be dominated by one or a few individuals.

6. Minutes of the meeting should be recorded and distributed to all members for agreement. To prevent misunderstandings later on, it might be a good idea for the chairperson to summarise decisions or actions for the minutes during the course of the meeting.

Team Briefing

As the name suggests, team briefing is when a manager or supervisor holds a short meeting with their staff to brief them on work-related issues. The team brief might be to explain a new process, review target figures or to remind employees of certain office procedures. Team briefing should not be a one-way communication process but one that encourages employees to give feedback to managers. Managers can use this information to gauge reaction to certain proposed initiatives or feed into future decision making. The nature of the work and size of work force will dictate how often team briefings are held. Team briefings may take place once a month following a management meeting or they may occur at the start of every shift.

Staff Suggestions

Employees should be encouraged to communicate suggestions to management. Suggestions made by employees may prove to be beneficial to the organisation. This can also provide valuable insight into how workers feel about their jobs and the organisation.

Chapter 12

DISPUTE RESOLUTION: DEALING WITH DISPUTES AT WORK

In Ireland, the primary responsibility for employment relations lies with management and employees. The system is voluntary in nature, which means that the government tends to stay out of negotiations and disputes as far as possible. With appropriate policies and procedures in place, most disputes can be solved without the need for third-party intervention. The state has provided a number of agencies to deal with employment relations problems that cannot be resolved within the organisation.

This chapter will help you to:

- recognise the importance of grievance and disciplinary procedures in preventing disputes
- draw up codes of practice for grievance and disciplinary procedures
- identify the main state resolution facilities that exist
- understand the functions of the Labour Court, the Labour Relations Commission (LRC), the Employment Appeals Tribunal (EAT) and the Equality Tribunal.

GRIEVANCE PROCEDURES

When an employee expresses their dissatisfaction with some aspect of their employment, this is called a grievance. Every organisation should have a grievance procedure in place so that employees know what steps they can take to have grievances addressed. Gunnigle, Heraty and Morley (1997) point out that the main aim of grievance procedures is to ensure that issues raised by employees are dealt with promptly and fairly, to avoid both the spread of dissent among workers and the escalation of the grievance into a serious industrial dispute. You need to clarify who the grievance should be raised with first (for example immediate manager or supervisor) and outline where the grievance should be referred if it is not resolved at the initial stage. You should aim to settle grievances fairly and as quickly as possible.

Suggestions for Handling a Grievance

* Consider handling the matter on an informal basis first.
* Make sure that the employee has the opportunity to explain their grievance.
* Establish all the facts pertaining to the grievance.
* Define the problem and seek clarification if necessary.
* Consider all appropriate evidence, factors and circumstances.
* Be objective at all stages of the procedure.
* Remember that the employee has the right to be represented.
* Maintain a record at all stages of the procedure.
* Refer the grievance to the next level of the procedure if necessary.
* Provide a right to appeal.

DISCIPLINARY PROCEDURES

When an employer is not satisfied with the work performance, behaviour or attitude of an employee, disciplinary action may be necessary. Every organisation should have a disciplinary procedure that informs employees of the consequences of not conforming to the rules and standards. These rules and standards and the penalties that can be imposed must be clearly defined and consistently applied. Employers are obliged to inform workers of the disciplinary procedure.

Suggestions for Handling Disciplinary Issues

* Consider handling the matter on an informal basis first.
* Discuss allegations or complaints with the employee concerned.
* Consider all appropriate evidence, factors and circumstances.
* Allow the employee the opportunity to respond fully to any allegations or complaints.
* Be objective at all stages of the disciplinary procedure.
* Remember that the employee has the right to be represented.
* Make sure the employee understands the reason for disciplinary action.

* Be fair and consistent with any action taken against the employee.

* Maintain a record at all stages of the procedure.

* Issue a warning to the employee if appropriate.

* Refer the issue to the next level of the procedure if necessary.

* Provide a right to appeal.

The disciplinary action imposed depends on the seriousness of the issue and may include:

* an oral warning

* a written warning

* a final written warning

* suspension without pay

* transfer to another task or section of the organisation

* demotion

* some other appropriate disciplinary action

* dismissal.

Good grievance and disciplinary procedures are important so that cases can be dealt with fairly and consistently. By following these procedures, your organisation may be able to deal with its own industrial relations problems without resorting to the state dispute resolution facilities. Moreover, if an action is taken against your organisation in the Labour Court, LRC or EAT, your grievance and disciplinary procedures will be examined and may influence the outcome of the action.

Employee participation in drawing up these procedures is advised and increases the likelihood that the procedures will be accepted. The procedures should be in writing and presented in language that is clearly understood. All employees should receive a copy of the procedures when they commence employment. Grievance and disciplinary procedures need to be updated regularly in line with any change of circumstances in the workplace and developments in employment legislation.

State Dispute Resolution Facilities

Employers and employees are encouraged to sort out their differences themselves. Where this is not possible, third party intervention may be required. This chapter focuses on the following state dispute resolution facilities:

* The Labour Court
* The Labour Relations Commission
* The Employment Appeals Tribunal
* The Office of the Director of Equality Investigations – The Equality Tribunal (ODEI).

The Labour Court

The Labour Court was established by the Industrial Relations Act, 1946 and today provides a free service for resolving disputes about:

- industrial relations
- equality
- organisation of working time
- national minimum wage.

Structure of the Labour Court

The Labour Court consists of nine full-time members: a chairperson, two deputy chairpersons and six ordinary members, three of whom are employers' members and three of whom are workers' members. The chairperson and two deputy chairpersons are appointed by the Minister for Enterprise, Trade and Employment. The employers' members are nominated by IBEC and the workers' members are nominated by ICTU.

The court operates in three separate divisions and each division is made up of the chair or a deputy chair, one employers' member and one workers' member. Sometimes the full court may be required to deal with certain issues.

The Process

The Labour Court is known as the "court of last resort". This means that the parties involved should try to resolve the dispute within their organisation or else through the LRC or the Rights Commissioner Service before coming to the Labour Court.

A case can arrive before the Labour Court in one of the following ways:

- referred by the LRC

- to appeal the decision of a rights commissioner
- to appeal the decision of the Director of Equality Investigations
- directly to the Labour Court
- at the request of the Minister for Enterprise, Trade and Employment.

When a case has been correctly referred to the Labour Court, the parties involved will be allocated a date and venue as soon as possible. Cases are usually heard in Dublin, but the Labour Court also holds hearings at a number of venues around the country. Each party must supply the Court with written submissions stating their positions in relation to the dispute. During the hearing, more information can be added to the written submission and members of the Court ask questions to clarify the situation. Hearings are usually held in private unless one of the parties requests that it be held in public.

After the hearing, the Labour Court will issue a written recommendation of how the dispute might be resolved, usually within three weeks. The Labour Court is not a court of law and its recommendations are generally not legally binding. The recommendation is offered as a third view and is expected to be considered seriously. An example of a case where the recommendation was not accepted was during the nurses' dispute in 2000. The Labour Court recommended that the nurses should accept the offer made to them, but the nurses opted to go on strike.

The Labour Court makes legally binding orders in cases where:

- employment legislation or registered employment agreements are breached
- the case is an appeal against the decision of a rights commissioner or an equality officer
- workers or unions agree to be bound by the Labour Court's recommendation.

In addition, the Labour Court has new powers to issue binding recommendations on pay and conditions where union recognition does not exist.

In 2002, the Labour Court received 940 referrals and held 590 hearings. There was an increase in the number of referrals under equality, industrial relations and organisation of working time legislation. A significant number of cases arose as a result of dismissal during pregnancy. In all such cases completed in 2002, the Labour Court found in favour of the complainant and awarded between $6,000 and $15,000 in compensation. For more information on the work carried out by the Labour Court during 2002, see the annual report on the Labour Court website.

The Labour Relations Commission (LRC)

The Labour Relations Commission was set up in 1991 under the Industrial Relations Act, 1990 to take over some of the responsibilities of the Labour Court. Its main functions are:

• to resolve disputes through its conciliation service

• to provide an industrial relations advisory service to employers, workers and trade unions

• to carry out research on industrial relations

• to provide a Rights Commissioner Service

• to prepare codes of practice

• to offer guidance on codes of practice.

The main work of the LRC is its conciliation service. Conciliation is a voluntary mediation process and the parties involved in a dispute are encouraged to take responsibility for its resolution. An industrial relations officer facilitates the resolution process by assisting the parties to find a mutually acceptable solution to their problems. The Industrial Relations Officer (IRO) first meets both parties together and then meets each party separately.

The principal aim of the LRC advisory, development and research service is to prevent industrial disputes from arising by helping employers and employees to build good relationships. It assists organisations in developing effective industrial relations practices, procedures and structures.

The LRC has responsibility for the Rights Commissioner Service that operates as an independent service of the Commission. The Rights Commissioner Service was originally the responsibility of the Labour Court but is now attached to the LRC. Rights commissioners are appointed by the Minister for Enterprise, Trade and Employment. They investigate the disputes, grievances and claims of individuals or small groups of workers regarding areas of legislation such as unfair dismissals, payment of wages, maternity, young persons, holidays and minimum pay.

Investigations are conducted in private. The rights commissioner's recommendation or decision can be appealed to the Labour Court or the Employment Appeals Tribunal, depending on the type of dispute.

The LRC has prepared the following codes of practice:

• procedures for addressing bullying in the workplace

• dispute procedures

- voluntary dispute resolution
- duties and responsibilities of employee representatives
- grievance and disciplinary procedures.

These codes of practice are intended to give *guidance* to employers and trade unions on particular issues. They are not legally enforceable.

The Employment Appeals Tribunal (EAT)

The EAT was established in 1967. It hears disputes in relation to legislation such as:

- unfair dismissal
- redundancy payment
- minimum notice
- maternity protection
- payment of wages
- terms of employment
- protection of young persons
- part-time workers.

Structure of the EAT

The Tribunal consists of a chairperson, twelve vice-chairpersons and forty ordinary members from ICTU and Employers' Associations. It acts in divisions of three, the chairperson or a vice-chairperson as well as two ordinary members, one from ICTU and one from Employers' Associations. Members of the EAT are appointed by the Minister for Enterprise, Trade and Employment.

The Process

Most cases have to go to the rights commissioner first, but cases regarding redundancy or minimum notice go directly to the EAT. Once an application to the EAT has been received by the Tribunal Office, a copy of the application will be sent to the employer concerned. The employer will be asked to respond within fourteen days. It may be six months before a date for the hearing is decided and each party may bring witnesses to the hearing to give evidence on their behalf. The parties involved can represent themselves, or have a solicitor or a representative from their trade union or employers' association. The Tribunal is usually held in public but can be held in private in some situations. The Tribunal's determination is sent in writing a few weeks after the hearing.

The Equality Tribunal (ODEI)

Established in 1999, the Equality Tribunal investigates and mediates claims of unlawful discrimination on nine grounds (discussed in Chapter 13 under the heading "Employment Equality").

The Investigation Process

* An employee, a representative or an Equality Authority refers a claim of discrimination to the Equality Tribunal.

* An investigation is carried out by a Tribunal Equality Officer.

* The decision of an Equality Officer is binding and enforceable by law. It is issued in writing after the hearing, normally contains full reasons and is required to be published.

* Decisions can be appealed to the Labour Court.

The Mediation Process

This is an alternative to the investigation process and it is carried out by an Equality Mediation Officer. The process is voluntary and can be terminated by either party at any time. Mediation agreements are binding but cannot be published. If there is no agreement, the investigation process may resume.

FURTHER INFORMATION

The following websites provide excellent, detailed information that will supplement what you have read in this chapter:

- www.labourcourt.ie

- www.lrc.ie

- www.entemp.ie

- www.odei.ie

Explanatory booklets relevant to the content of this chapter are available, free of charge, from Citizen Information Centres.

CONTACT

Rights Commissioner
Tom Johnson House
Haddington Road
Dublin 4
Tel: (01) 613 6700 or lo call 1890 220 227

Labour Court
Tom Johnson House
Haddington Road
Dublin 4
Tel: (01) 613 6666 or lo call 1890 220 228
e-mail: info@labourcourt.ie
www.labourcourt.ie

Labour Relations Commission
Tom Johnson House
Haddington Road
Dublin 4
Tel: (01) 613 6700 or lo call 1890 220 227
www.lrc.ie

Employment Appeals Tribunal
Davitt House
65A Adelaide Road
Dublin 2
Tel: (01) 631 3006

Department of Enterprise, Trade and Employment
Davitt House
65A Adelaide Road
Dublin 2
Tel: (01) 631 2121 or lo call 1890 220 222
www.entemp.ie

Office of the Director of Equality Investigations – The Equality Tribunal
3 Clonmel Street
Harcourt Street
Dublin 2
Tel: (01) 477 4100 or lo call 1890 344 424
e-mail: info@odei.ie
www.odei.ie

Chapter 13

EMPLOYMENT LEGISLATION: UNDERSTANDING THE LAW[1]

"The principal purpose of labour law is to regulate, to support and to restrain the power of management and the power of organised labour."

(Kahn-Freund, 1977)

In other words, employment legislation provides a framework within which the worker–employer relationship can be structured. It is necessary for all employers and managers to be familiar with current employment legislation in order to comply with their legal obligations.

This chapter will help you to:

- understand the legal obligations of employers towards their employees

- distinguish between a contract *of* service and a contract *for* service

- draft a "Terms of Employment" statement

- understand the laws and cases relating to terms of employment, wages, dismissal, redundancy, equality, maternity, health and safety, holidays, hours of work and rest breaks, young workers, minimum notice, part-time workers, minimum wage and pensions.

EMPLOYEE STATUS

It is important to distinguish between a *contract of service* and a *contract for service*. An "employee" is employed under a contract *of* service, whereas an "independent contractor" is employed under a contract *for* service. This distinction is important because only those under a contract *of* service have statutory protection, for example the right to claim unfair dismissal or maternity leave. Furthermore, employees under a contract of service are entitled to preference for payment when a company is

---

[1] This chapter summarises many of the principal provisions of employment legislation in Ireland. The information provided is for guidance purposes only and is not intended to be a complete or authoritative statement of the law.

winding up. The legal distinction between an employee and an independent contractor is not always obvious. Problems can arise, for example, with pension entitlements or redundancy payment.

The following questions are among those considered by the courts when deciding the status of a particular worker:

* Does the employer have the right to tell the individual *how* to carry out the work?

* Is the individual integrated into, or part of, the employer's business?

* Is the individual paid a wage/salary or a fee?

* Are income tax and social insurance deducted by the organisation or by the individual?

* Are tools and equipment provided by the organisation or by the individual?

* Is the worker free to work for other organisations?

TERMS OF EMPLOYMENT

Relevant legislation: Terms of Employment (Information) Act, 1994 and 2001

When a person is offered employment in return for wages, and accepts the offer, a contract of employment comes into existence. The contract of employment does not have to be in writing but the Terms of Employment (Information) Act states that certain terms of the contract must be available to the employee in writing within two months of taking up employment. This written statement must include:

• full names and addresses of employer and employee

• place of work

• job title or nature of work

• date of commencement of employment

• nature of contract (temporary or fixed term)

• details of pay and paid leave

• hours of work (including overtime) and details of rest breaks

• period of notice to be given by employer and employee.

Some employers also provide details on rules and regulations, grievance procedures and disciplinary procedures. Employees may be referred to other documents, such as policy documents or the staff handbook, for additional information.

The legislation referred to sets out the minimum to which an employee is entitled, such as minimum pay, minimum notice, holiday time and maternity leave. An employee's contract may provide for greater entitlements than the statutory minimum, but not less.

The employee has the right to complain to a rights commissioner if the employer fails to provide a written statement in accordance with The Terms of Employment Act or fails to notify the employee of changes in the statement.

WAGES

Relevant legislation: Payment of Wages Act, 1991

Employers are obliged to give each employee a written statement of gross wages itemising each deduction with every wage packet. Wages may be paid by cheque, credit transfer, cash, postal/money order or bank draft. Employers may not make deductions from wages unless required by law or with the written consent of the employee.

For the purposes of the Act, the following payments are regarded as wages:

- normal basic pay as well as any overtime entitlements
- shift allowances or other similar payments
- any fee, bonus or commission
- any holiday, sick or maternity pay
- any other payment for work
- any sum payable to an employee in lieu of notice of termination of employment.

Complaints may be referred to a rights commissioner.

Dismissal

Relevant legislation: The Unfair Dismissals Acts, 1977–2001
Redundancy Payments Acts, 1967–2003

The purpose of the Unfair Dismissals Acts is to protect employees from being unfairly dismissed from their employment. An employee who is dismissed from their employment can bring a claim for unfair dismissal against their employer once they have been in that employment for at least a year. The employee must be employed under a contract *of* service.

Unfair Dismissals

The Act states that a dismissal will be automatically "unfair" if it can be attributed to:

- trade union membership or activity
- religious or political opinion
- involvement in civil or criminal legal proceedings against the employer
- race or colour
- sexual orientation
- age
- unfair selection for redundancy
- taking maternity, adoptive, parental or carer's leave
- an employee exercising their right to a minimum wage
- being a member of the travelling community
- pregnancy.

The requirement to have one year's continuous service does not apply if the dismissal can be attributed to one of the following:

- pregnancy or for taking maternity leave, parental leave or adoptive leave
- an employee exercising their rights under the National Minimum Wage Act, 2000
- an employee taking carer's leave
- trade union membership or activity.

White v Simon Betson (1992)   The claimant maintained that although his weekly wage had been agreed when he started work, he was paid irregular amounts at regular intervals. He became a member of SIPTU, which wrote to the employer requesting a discussion on the claimant's conditions of employment. The claimant was dismissed after returning from sick leave. The Employment Appeals Tribunal found that the claimant had been dismissed as a result of trade union membership.

Merriman v St James Hospital (1986)   A hospital attendant was dismissed because she refused, on religious grounds, to bring a crucifix and candle to a dying patient. The Circuit Court held that this was an unfair dismissal.

Raouf Malek v Interactive Services (2003)   Mr Malek worked as a software tester for Interactive Services and achieved a score well above average in an appraisal test. The criteria that the firm had in place for making staff redundant were based on performance at the last employee appraisal review. The Employment Appeals Tribunal ruled that Mr Malek was unfairly selected for redundancy. He was awarded €12,000.

Dillon v Wexford Seamless Aluminium Gutters (1980)   The court found that the employee was unfairly selected for redundancy due to trade union activities.

Maxwell v English Language Institute (1990)   A secretary submitted a maternity allowance claim form to her employer, who did not complete it. When she informed her employer that she was planning to take maternity leave, she was dismissed. The employer claimed that her work was unsatisfactory but the Employment Appeals Tribunal found that she had been dismissed because of her pregnancy.

Constructive Dismissal

An employee who leaves a job, rather than being dismissed, may still have a claim for unfair dismissal. Constructive dismissal occurs when an employee leaves the workplace but is treated as having been dismissed, because the employer's conduct has made it impossible for the employee to stay. In this case, the burden of proof lies with the employee.

Liz Allen v Independent Newspapers (2001)   Liz Allen was a crime correspondent with the Sunday Independent newspaper. She took a case of constructive dismissal against her employers, Independent Newspapers, because the treatment she received from some of her colleagues forced her to leave. She felt she had no option but to resign because she had been isolated and bullied at work and her confidence and health had been undermined. She won her case and was awarded over £70,000 (€88,882) in compensation. The Equality Authority made the award on the basis that the defendants had not taken action on the complaints she had made over a two-year period.

Employees Excluded from the Act

All employees are covered by the Acts except those:

• with less than one year's continuous service

• over the normal retiring age

• employed by the Defence Forces and the Garda Síochána

• employed by the state

• employed by a close relative in a private house or farm where both parties live

• FÁS trainees and apprentices.

These exclusions from the Act do not apply where dismissal results from the employee's pregnancy or taking maternity leave, adoptive leave, parental leave or carer's leave.

The Unfair Dismissal Acts do not cover employees on fixed-term or fixed-purpose contracts who are let go when the contract expires or the purpose ceases, provided the contract, signed by both parties, specifies that the Unfair Dismissals Acts do not apply. If a break between contracts of less than three months is deemed to have been introduced so that the employer could avoid liability under the Acts, the contracts will be added together to calculate continuous service of an employee.

An unfair dismissals action can be brought by an employee to a rights commissioner or the EAT within six months of dismissal, or twelve months in exceptional circumstances. Either party may appeal the Tribunal's decision to the circuit court within six weeks. Certain unfair dismissal cases are dealt with by the Labour Court under equality legislation.

In cases of unfair dismissal, the burden of proof usually lies with the employer. This means that, in general, every dismissal of an employee will be presumed to be unfair unless the employer can prove that the dismissal was justified.

Employees who feel that they have been unfairly dismissed but who do not qualify under the Unfair Dismissals Acts (for example if they have less than one year's continuous service) may, in most cases, refer the matter to a rights commissioner.

Fair Dismissal

Employers have the right to dismiss workers in certain circumstances. These can be discussed under the following headings:

- conduct
- capability
- competence
- qualifications
- redundancy.

Conduct

An employee can be dismissed for conduct such as sick leave abuse, substance or alcohol abuse, dishonesty, criminal convictions, conflict of interest, disobedience and violence. This can apply to conduct outside one's place of employment.

> *Flynn v Sisters of Holy Faith* (1985)   A secondary school teacher who had a baby with a married man was dismissed following complaints from parents. The case went to the EAT, the Circuit Court and the High Court and the teacher was found to have been fairly dismissed because her conduct violated her obligations to the Catholic ethos of the school.

> *Hardy v Cadbury Ireland Ltd* (1983)   The employee was found to have been working for somebody else while out on sick leave. The Tribunal upheld the dismissal.

Capability

An employee can be dismissed if they do not have either the mental or the physical capability to do the job.

> *Guru v The Office of Public Works* (1990)   The Tribunal found that
> there is no obligation on the employer to provide light work or alter-
> native duties for an employee who is no longer capable of carrying
> out their duties.

Competence

An employee can be dismissed on the basis of competence. Poor work
performance, substandard work and persistent lateness or absenteeism
are justifiable reasons for dismissal.

> *Dixon v H. Williams and Co. Ltd* (1981)   A shop assistant who was
> absent due to illness was found to be fairly dismissed, as attendance
> was poor over a period and appropriate warnings were given.

Qualifications

An employee can be dismissed if they do not have the qualifications
necessary to do the job. An employee whose job description includes
driving a vehicle could be dismissed if they lost their driving licence.

> *Ryder and Byrne v Commissioners of Irish Lights* (1980)   The em-
> ployer required two members of staff to obtain higher technical quali-
> fications within a reasonable time. They failed to comply with the
> requirement and were dismissed. The Tribunal upheld the dismissal.

Redundancy

An employee can be made redundant if the organisation is ceasing business or reducing its workforce. A worker may contest redundancy on
the grounds of unfair selection for dismissal.

Redundancy Payment

According to the Redundancy Payments Acts, 1967–2003, an employee
employed by the organisation for two years is entitled to the following
redundancy payment:

• two weeks' pay for each year in the employment

• one week's additional pay.

Employers are entitled to a rebate of 60 per cent from the Department of

Enterprise, Trade and Employment, provided they have given the employee two weeks' notice and have paid the statutory redundancy.

Employers' Obligations

When a case is referred to the EAT, the tribunal will try to assess whether the employer dealt with the situation in a reasonable manner. The Unfair Dismissals Acts, 1977–2001 require employers to give notice in writing to each employee explaining the organisation's dismissal procedure. This information must be given within 28 days of entering into a contract of employment.

Fennell and Lynch (1993) have identified four basic obligations of employers with regard to the procedures involved in dismissing an employee. These are:

1. *Investigation*: the employer needs to show that the matter was investigated fairly before a decision was made to dismiss the individual.

2. *Hearing*: the employee must be given an opportunity to respond and should be allowed to have trade union representation at this meeting.

3. *Warning*: as far as possible, the employee should be given a warning and an opportunity to improve.

4. *Proportionate penalties*: the Tribunal decides whether dismissal was fair and in proportion to the behaviour of the employee.

An employer who has dismissed an employee must, if asked, give the employee the reasons for dismissal in writing within fourteen days.

Unfair Dismissal Remedies

The tribunal may decide an employee was unfairly dismissed and assess the extent to which each party was at fault. This decision affects the remedy chosen.

Reinstatement is the return of the employee to their previous job with back pay. It is as if the dismissal never took place and the employee must benefit from any improvement in terms and conditions of employment that may have occurred between the date of dismissal and the date of reinstatement.

Re-engagement allows the employee to return to their previous job or a similar job, usually without back pay.

Compensation is the most common remedy and has a maximum of 104 weeks' pay. It may be given in addition to the other remedies or on its own. An employee found to have been unfairly dismissed but who has suffered no financial loss may be awarded up to four weeks' pay.

EMPLOYMENT EQUALITY

Relevant legislation: The Employment Equality Act, 1998

This legislation protects employees against discrimination at work on nine distinct grounds:

1. gender

2. marital status

3. family status

4. sexual orientation

5. religious belief

6. age

7. disability

8. race

9. membership of the travelling community.

Employees are protected from discrimination with regard to recruitment advertising, employment, conditions of employment, training and promotion.

Gleeson v Rotunda and Mater Hospitals (2000)   In this case of gender discrimination, Dr Noreen Gleeson was awarded €63,500. When she was being interviewed for a job, she was asked about the time she "had her babies". The Labour Court found that Ms Gleeson was better qualified and more experienced than the successful applicant.

Freeman v Superquinn (2002)   In March 2002, Superquinn was ordered to pay €20,000 in compensation to an employee at one if its Dublin stores who was discriminated against on the grounds of age, marital and family status when she applied for the post of head cashier. It was the first case to be won on the marital status and family status grounds under the Employment Equality Act, 1998.

Dr Bennet Eng v St James' Hospital (2002)   In December 2001, the Office of Director of Equality Investigations found that St James' Hospital discriminated against Dr Bennet Eng on racial grounds. It was found to be unlawful for Dr Eng to work as an intern without a basic salary when his Irish colleagues were in salaried positions. The case was appealed to the Labour Court in May 2002 and the decision of the Equality Officer was upheld.

A worker v A company (2002)   A claimant with Cerebral Palsy was asked to carry out tasks that she found difficult due to her disability. She left her job and contended she had been constructively dismissed. She was awarded €9,000 in January 2002, when the Labour Court found that her employer had not done "all that is reasonable to accommodate the needs of a person with a disability".

Maguire v NE Health Board   The Equality Officer found that a temporary care attendant was treated differently by staff and management when they discovered that he was a traveller. The Equality Officer also found that management had failed in its obligations to investigate the complaint. The NE Health Board was ordered to implement a Harassment Policy and to pay the claimant €5,000 for stress suffered.

Complaints may be directed to the ODEI (The Equality Tribunal) within six months. Dismissals or resignations arising from the Employment Equality Act provisions may be referred directly to the Labour Court, while complaints in relation to gender discrimination may be referred directly to the Circuit Court.

Note The Equality Authority provides grants to help put equality policies in place and to develop and implement quality training in the workplace. See www.equality.ie for more information.

MATERNITY LEAVE

Relevant legislation: Maternity Protection Acts, 1994 and 2001

This legislation sets out the main entitlements and obligations of pregnant employees:

• all employees are protected, regardless of period of service or number of hours worked per week

- the employee is allowed to attend certain ante- and post-natal medical visits without loss of pay

- the employee is entitled to eighteen weeks' paid leave, four of which must be taken before the birth and four after

- maternity benefit of up to 70 per cent of income is paid by the Department of Social Community and Family Affairs (some organisations supplement the maternity benefit)

- the employee may take up to eight weeks' unpaid leave

- the employee must give four weeks' notice before going on maternity leave as well as presenting a medical certificate

- the employee must notify the organisation in writing at least four weeks in advance of her return.

Disputes concerning any of the above entitlements may be referred to a rights commissioner within six months.

HEALTH AND SAFETY

According to the Health and Safety Authority's annual report, 61 people died from workplace injuries in Ireland in 2002. Of these deaths, 21 occurred in the construction industry and 13, including 2 children, occurred in farm accidents. An estimated 1.4 million days were lost due to workplace injury or illness in 2002.

Relevant legislation: The Safety, Health and Welfare at Work Act, 1989
The Safety, Health and Welfare at Work (General Application) Regulations, 1993

According to this legislation, employers are primarily responsible for creating and maintaining a safe and healthy work environment. Every employer must provide a safe workplace and is required to prepare a safety statement for the workplace. This statement should identify any hazards that exist and outline the measures that are to be taken to deal with these risks.

Employees are also responsible for health and safety at work and must be consulted on any matters dealing with health and safety in the workplace. Employees are obliged to wear protective equipment when necessary and to take care when using machinery, tools and potentially dangerous substances.

Oran Pre-Cast Concrete (2003)   In July 2003, Oran Pre-Cast Concrete Limited was fined €500,000 for breaches of health and safety legislation. The conviction followed an investigation by the Health and Safety Authority into the death of a 25-year-old man in an accident at work. The employee fell from a height of nine metres while replacing a damaged roof gutter on a building. The man who died had not received adequate safety training for the height at which he was working when the accident happened.

The Early Learning Centre (2003)   In January 2003, The Early Learning Centre store in Galway was fined €600 for breaches of health and safety legislation. Staff members had not received adequate training or instruction in manual handling. In addition, the company did not have a safety statement for its Eyre Square store as required under health and safety legislation.

Kilkishen Homes (2003)   In January 2003, a director of Kilkishen Homes was jailed for contempt of court in relation to non-compliance with safety standards.

Roadstone Dublin Limited (2003)   In February 2003, Roadstone Dublin Limited was fined €12,000 following a serious accident that resulted in an employee's left hand being amputated. Costs and expenses were awarded to the Health and Safety Authority.

Tara Mines Ltd (2002)   In November 2002, Tara Mines Ltd was fined €3,808 for breaches of health and safety legislation following an accident where an employee lost his right eye. The company had failed to include an assessment of the risks associated with a particular machine in their safety statement. Costs were awarded to the Health and Safety Authority.

For issues regarding health and safety, contact the Health and Safety Authority. See www.hsa.ie for more information.

HOLIDAYS

Relevant legislation: The Organisation of Working Time Act, 1997

Annual Leave

* All employees are entitled to at least twenty days' annual leave.

* All employees are entitled to an unbroken period of two weeks' annual leave once they have worked for eight months.

* Holiday pay can be calculated as 8 per cent of hours worked in a leave year.

* Calculation of holidays should include overtime, time spent on annual leave, maternity leave, parental leave, force majeure leave, adoptive leave and time spent on the first thirteen weeks of carer's leave.

* Part-time, temporary and casual employees have an entitlement to 8 per cent of hours worked.

* Holiday pay is paid in advance at the normal weekly rate.

* A day of sickness during holidays which is covered by a medical certificate is not counted as annual leave.

Public Holidays

* Employees are entitled to nine public holidays every year (Christmas Day, St Stephen's Day, New Year's Day, St Patrick's Day, Easter Monday, the first Mondays in May, June and August, the last Monday in October) and the employer must provide one of the following:
  - a paid day off on the public holiday
  - a paid day off within a month of the public holiday
  - a specified Church holiday falling immediately before or after the public holiday in lieu
  - an additional day of annual leave
  - an additional day's pay if an employee works on the public holiday.

* The employer must inform the employee which of these alternatives will apply at least two weeks before the public holiday takes place.

* There is no service requirement in respect of public holidays for full-time employees.

* Part-time employees are only entitled to a public holiday if they have

worked at least 40 hours during the 5 weeks immediately prior to the public holiday falling.

- If the public holiday falls on a day on which the employee does not normally work, the employee is entitled to one-fifth of their normal weekly wage for the day, a paid day off within a month or an extra day's annual leave.

When an employee leaves the organisation, they are entitled to be paid any holiday leave due to them either in the current leave year or in the previous one. The employer must keep records of holidays and public holidays for at least three years to show that the Act is being complied with.

> *L. Patchell v Prime News Ltd* (2002)   The Labour Court determined that Ms Patchell, a part-time worker, should be paid a total of €1,376.56 in respect of unpaid annual leave and public holiday entitlement.

> *Gerry Kelly Enterprises Limited v Andris Reinfelds* (2002)   In 2002, a bricklayer who was not paid for public holidays or annual leave to which he was entitled was awarded €345 compensation for loss of holiday pay and €1,000 additional compensation.

Complaints in relation to holiday entitlements may be directed to a rights commissioner within six months of the dispute occurring.

HOURS OF WORK AND REST BREAKS

Relevant legislation: The Organisation of Working Time Act, 1997

Maximum Weekly Working Time

The maximum average working week is 48 hours. Averaging may be balanced out over a four-, six- or twelve-month period depending on the circumstances.

Zero Hours

When an employee is requested to be available for work but then is not needed, they are entitled to be paid for either 25 per cent of the time that they were required to be available or fifteen hours, whichever is less. For example, if an employee is asked to be available to work eight hours and is not called in to work, the employee will be entitled to a minimum payment of two hours. An employee must be informed at least twenty-four hours in advance of starting and finishing times or any other changes in working times.

Rest Breaks

Every employee has a general entitlement to:

- a daily rest break of eleven consecutive hours
- fifteen minutes where more than four and a half hours have been worked
- thirty minutes where more than six hours have been worked, which may include the first break
- shop employees whose hours of work include the hours 11.30 am to 2.30 pm must be allowed a break of one hour after six hours' work commencing between the hours of 11.30 am and 2.30 pm
- night workers whose work involves special hazards or a heavy physical or mental strain can work a maximum of eight hours in a twenty-four hour period.

Complaints may be directed to a rights commissioner.

Young Workers

Relevant legislation: The Protection of Young Persons (Employment) Act, 1996

- Children over fourteen can do light work outside school term for no more than seven hours in any day or thirty-five in any week.
- Children over fifteen, but under sixteen, may work up to eight hours a week doing light work during school term time.
- Children under sixteen may not work between 8 pm and 8 am.
- Young persons, i.e. between the ages of sixteen and eighteen, may work for a maximum of eight hours in one day or forty hours in one week.
- Young persons may not be employed between the hours of 10 pm and 6 am.
- The employer is obliged to see the birth certificate of employees under

eighteen and to get written permission from the parents or guardian of employees under sixteen.

* Employers who employ young people under the age of eighteen must give a summary of the act to the employee.

> *Supermac's* (2003) In February 2003, the Loughrea branch of Supermac's fast food restaurant was fined €3,400 for allowing two seventeen-year-old students to work after 10 pm.

Complaints may be directed to a rights commissioner.

MINIMUM NOTICE

Relevant legislation: Minimum Notice and Terms of Employment Act, 1973–1991

Once an employee has worked for thirteen weeks in a job, they are entitled to notice before the employer may dismiss them. The minimum notice provided for is:

Table 13.1: Minimum Notice

Duration of employment	Minimum notice
13 weeks to 2 years	1 week
2 years to 5 years	2 weeks
5 years to 10 years	4 weeks
10 years to 15 years	6 weeks
15 years or more	8 weeks

The Act requires an employee to give an employer one week's notice of leaving, no matter how long they have been in that employment. However, a contract of employment may provide for a greater period of notice to be given by the employee.

If an employee is dismissed for "misconduct", the employer does not have to give any notice or payment in lieu of notice. The Employment Appeals Tribunal tends to include violence and theft as examples of misconduct, but may not include refusal by an employee to accept reasonable instructions, being late and so on.

Disputes concerning minimum notice may be referred to the Employment Appeals Tribunal.

PART-TIME WORKERS

Relevant legislation: Protection of Employees (Part-Time Work) Act, 2001

This Act came into effect on 20 December 2001 and specifies that part-time workers cannot be treated any less favourably than a "comparable" full-time employee when it comes to their conditions of employment such as pay, overtime, holidays, voluntary health contributions and entitlement to sick pay. Part-time workers who work at least 20 per cent of the normal hours of the comparable full-time employee are entitled to any pension schemes or arrangements that are enjoyed by full-time employees.

Disputes concerning part-time workers' legislation may be referred to a rights commissioner.

MINIMUM WAGE

Relevant legislation: National Minimum Wage Act, 2000

In April 2000, the national minimum wage came into effect. At that time, employees, with some exceptions, were guaranteed a minimum wage of €5.59/hour. There is a provision in the legislation for this figure to be reviewed at regular intervals and already there have been two increases. The minimum wage was raised to €5.97/hour from July 2001, €6.35/hour in October 2002 and will be increased to €7/hour in February 2004.

Employees under the age of eighteen are only guaranteed up to 70 per cent of the national minimum wage. In the first year after the date of first employment over age eighteen, 80 per cent of the national minimum wage is guaranteed and in the second year, 90 per cent. This also applies to over eighteens who enter employment for the first time.

Certain employees who are over eighteen and undergoing a course of training or study authorised by the employer are only guaranteed a reduced national minimum wage.

Ivory Hotel v Rita Gedminaite   In a case against the Ivory Hotel in Waterford in 2002, a claimant was awarded €1,047 arrears of wages under the National Minimum Wage Act, 2000.

An employee may request an inspector from the Department of Enterprise, Trade and Employment to investigate a claim that the national minimum wage is not being paid. An employer in financial difficulty can contact the Labour Court to apply for a temporary exemption from paying the minimum wage. An employer must keep all necessary records for three years to show that the Act is being complied with.

PENSIONS

Relevant legislation: The Pensions (Amendment) Act, 2002

From 15 September 2003, all employers in Ireland are obliged to provide access to at least one standard personal retirement savings account (PRSA) for their employees. This means that employers must provide the facility to deduct contributions from an employee's pay and transfer it to a pension plan if that employee wishes to be part of a pension scheme. The employer can choose the PRSA provider(s) but does not have to contribute to the PRSA on behalf of an employee.

Table 13.2: Summary of Principal Employment Legislation

* Terms of Employment (Information) Act (1994 and 2001)
* Payment of Wages Act (1991)
* Unfair Dismissals Act (1977–2001)
* Redundancy Payments Act (1967–2003)
* Employment Equality Act (1998)
* Maternity Protection Act (1994 and 2001)
* Safety, Health and Welfare at Work Act (1989)
* Safety, Health and Welfare at Work (General Application) Regulations (1993)
* Organisation of Working Time Act (1997)
* Protection of Young Persons (Employment) Act (1996)
* Minimum Notice and Terms of Employment Act (1973–1991)
* Protection of Employees (Part-Time Work) Act (2001)
* National Minimum Wage Act (2000)
* The Pensions (Amendment) Act (2002)

FURTHER INFORMATION

The following websites provide excellent, detailed information which will supplement what you have read in this chapter:

- www.comhairle.ie
- www.entemp.ie
- www.labourcourt.ie
- www.oasis.gov.ie
- www.hsa.ie (Health and Safety Authority)
- www.equality.ie (Equality Authority)

Explanatory booklets relevant to the content of this chapter are available, free of charge, from Citizens Information Centres.

CONTACT

Employment Rights Information Unit
Davitt House
65A Adelaide Road
Dublin 2
Tel: (01) 631 3131 or lo call 1890 201 615
e-mail: erinfo@entemp.ie

Chapter 14

Trade Unions and Employers' Associations

The notion that workers and management may have different objectives and need to protect their interests by showing a united front was raised in Chapter 1. Both trade unions and employers' associations represent groups of people protecting their own interests. Trade unions represent employees and employers' associations represent employers.

This chapter will help you to:

- understand the roles of trade unions and employers' associations in the employment relationship
- identify the main trade unions and employers' associations in Ireland
- be familiar with the typical structure of a trade union
- be aware of the functions of trade unions and employers' associations and the services they provide for their members.

Trade Unions

According to Gunnigle, Heraty and Morley (1997: 201), "trade unions may be viewed as permanent associations of organised employees" whose primary objectives are:

- to replace individual bargaining with collective bargaining
- to facilitate the development of a political system where workers' interests have a greater degree of influence on political decisions
- to achieve satisfactory levels of pay and conditions of employment
- to provide members with a range of services.

Legal Status

Every worker in Ireland has a constitutional right to be a member of a trade union. A worker who is a member of a trade union or involved in trade union activity is protected by laws such as the Unfair Dismissals

Act, 1977–2001 and the Employment Equality Act, 1998. However, organisations are not legally obliged to recognise any trade union and may refuse to negotiate with them.

For a group of workers to operate as a trade union, with a negotiating licence, there must be at least 1,000 members and a minimum deposit with the High Court of £20,000.

Types of Trade Union

Gunnigle, Heraty and Morley (1997) group trade unions in Ireland into three broad categories, pointing out that nowadays it may be difficult to slot individual unions into one particular category.

Craft unions were the first unions to be established in the mid-1800s. They represent skilled workers, such as carpenters, who had to serve an apprenticeship in their trade. At one time, craft unions had a lot of power because entry to the craft was controlled. In other words, only people who had completed a recognised apprenticeship and were union members were allowed to work in the trade. Because of technological developments in many areas of work, such as printing, the power of craft workers has decreased as their skills have become less valuable or even obsolete.

General unions have existed in Ireland since the 1860s but became more prominent in the early 1900s. The membership of general unions comprises workers from all occupations and industries. While traditionally, general unions catered for unskilled or semi-skilled workers, nowadays they also attract craft and white-collar workers too.

White-collar unions mostly cater for professional, supervisory, clerical and managerial workers. There has been a big increase in membership since the 1960s and this can be partly attributed to the growth of the service sector in Ireland. White-collar workers were not traditionally typical union members but may have been encouraged to become unionised by the success of general unions in improving pay and conditions for workers.

Typical Structure of a Union

The *shop steward* is an employee of the organisation who has been elected by co-workers to be the main trade union representative in the workplace, or in a particular section of the workplace. Shop stewards deal with employee grievances and inform members of union business, liaise with and support union officials and negotiate with management. Shop stewards are not paid for the work they do for the union but they are allowed a certain amount of time off work to carry out union duties.

A union *branch* is formed either by members from a number of smaller organisations or by members from one large organisation. The members of a branch are represented by a *branch committee*.

At national level, union officers are elected at the *annual delegates' conference*. A number of issues put forward by branches are discussed at the annual delegates' conference and this leads to the formulation of union policies. In this way, decisions are made regarding the issues the union will focus on. The *general officers* of the union are usually full-time union employees.

The Irish Congress of Trade Unions (ICTU)

The Irish Congress of Trade Unions is the umbrella organisation for trade unions in Ireland, to which 97 per cent of Irish trade unions are affiliated. A notable exception is the Association of Secondary Teachers of Ireland (ASTI), which decided to withdraw from the ICTU in January 2000 because members felt they could negotiate a better deal for pay and conditions independently. The main functions of the ICTU are to:

- co-ordinate the work of trade unions in Ireland
- represent the interests of workers, especially to government
- assist with the resolution of disputes between unions and employers
- promote trade unionism and trade union policies
- negotiate national agreements such as Sustaining Progress.

The ICTU is represented on government advisory bodies and, as you may remember from Chapter 10, it nominates representatives for appointment to a number of bodies including the Labour Court and the Labour Relations Commission.

ALTERNATIVES TO TRADE UNIONS

It must be pointed out that workers have the right *not* to be a member of a trade union if they so choose. The alternatives to trade union membership are individual bargaining and staff associations.

Individual bargaining involves each employee negotiating solely on their own behalf and the outcomes of negotiating pay, conditions or any other matters apply only to the individual and not across the board, as is the case with the collective bargaining carried out by unions.

Staff associations are often formed by workers within an organisation as an alternative to trade unions. Membership is confined to workers within the organisation, so compared to the bigger trade unions, staff associations have limited bargaining power. Staff associations are traditionally associated with professional and managerial staff.

Employers' Associations

Workers protect their interests by joining trade unions. Employers become members of employers' associations for similar reasons. Employers' associations provide for their members services similar to those provided by trade unions for their members. These services include:

- advising members on employment legislation and other matters relevant to human resource management

- carrying out research on, for example, economic trends and pay levels

- representing members in collective bargaining negotiations, at the Labour Court and at the Employment Appeals Tribunal

- representing members' views to the government, trade unions and the public

- providing training for members.

Irish Business and Employers Confederation (IBEC)

IBEC is the largest employers' association in Ireland. It was established on 1 January 1993 as the result of a merger between the Federation of Irish Employers (FIE) and the Confederation of Irish Industry (CII). Today, over 7,000 firms are members.

IBEC provides a wide range of services to individual member businesses and organisations from all sectors and of all sizes. The *Economic Affairs* division conducts economic research and provides information to members on all aspects of the economy. The *Social Policy Service* represents members' interests to government and others regarding proposed changes to employment legislation at EU and national level. It also informs and advises members on the effect changes will have on human resources. *The Industrial Relations/Human Resources* division provides a number of services to members, including mediation, management training and development, and advice, consultation and representation on all employment and industrial relations matters. In addition, IBEC has established a number of *Policy Committees*, which reflect infrastructure and government policy areas, which impact on the business agenda, including transport, energy and environment. IBEC represents Irish business and employers both nationally and internationally.

Other Employers' Associations

These associations cater for small and medium-sized organisations:

- Small Firms Association (SFA)
- Irish Small and Medium Enterprises Association (ISME).

Other employers' associations tend to be industry specific. Here are some examples:

- Construction Industry Federation (CIF)
- Irish Hotels Federation
- Society of the Irish Motor Industry (SIMI)
- Licensed Vintners' Association
- Irish Pharmaceutical Union.

FURTHER INFORMATION

The following websites provide excellent, detailed information that will supplement what you have read in this chapter:

- www.ibec.ie
- www.ictu.ie
- www.siptu.ie
- www.sfa.ie
- www.isme.ie

APPENDICES

Appendix 1

SAMPLE JOB APPLICATION FORM

PRIVATE & CONFIDENTIAL

XXX Limited

APPLICATION FORM

Please complete form in black ink or type

POSITION APPLIED FOR _____

PERSONAL DETAILS

Surname _____   Forenames _____

Preferred title: ☐ Mr / ☐ Mrs / ☐ Ms / ☐ Miss / ☐ Other (specify_____)

Address _____

_____

Telephone No.: Daytime _____   Evening _____

E-mail _____

Do you hold a current vehicle driving licence?   ☐ Yes / ☐ No

Type of licence: ☐ Full / ☐ Provisional / ☐ Other (specify_____)

EDUCATION, QUALIFICATIONS & TRAINING

DATE from/to mth/year	SCHOOL, COLLEGE, UNIVERSITY	QUALIFICATIONS GAINED	DATE PASSED

OTHER COURSES ATTENDED

DATE from/to mth/year	COURSE TITLE AND NAME OF ORGANISER	SUBJECTS	LENGTH OF COURSE

EMPLOYMENT DETAILS

Detail all __previous__ employment (including unpaid and voluntary work), starting with your current or most recent employer. If necessary continue on separate sheet.

DATE from/to mth/year	EMPLOYER	POSITION AND DUTIES	SALARY	REASON FOR LEAVING

INTERESTS

_____

_____

ADDITIONAL INFORMATION

Please supply any additional information that will assist in the assessment of your application.

_____

_____

_____

_____

REFEREES
Please provide the names of TWO people who may be approached for a reference in respect of your work experience. Please indicate if you do not wish your referees to be contacted at this stage.

Name _____   Name_____

Position _____   Position _____

Address _____   Address_____

_____   _____

_____   _____

Telephone No. _____   Telephone No. _____

Contact: ☐ Yes / ☐ No   Contact: ☐ Yes / ☐ No

I confirm that to the best of my knowledge and belief that all the particulars I have given on this application form are true and accurate. I understand that any inaccurate or false information given may result in an offer of employment being withdrawn.

NAME _____   DATE _____

Please return completed application form, marked Private & Confidential, to:

XXX Limited is an Equal Opportunities Employer

SAMPLE LETTER INVITING CANDIDATE TO INTERVIEW

Dear

Vacancy Job Title

Thank you for your recent application.

I would be grateful if you could attend this office for interview with
_____ on _____ at _____.

Options

- As part of the interview process, you will be required to ... (e.g. complete a test, make a presentation).

- I would be grateful if you could bring with you original evidence of qualifications.

I look forward to meeting you on_____. If you are unable to attend, please contact me by_____.

Yours sincerely,

_____

Name
Title

SAMPLE LETTER REJECTING APPLICATION

Dear

Vacancy Job Title

Thank you for your recent application.

We have now had an opportunity to review all applications and, after careful consideration, we regret to advise that we are unable to progress your application any further on this occasion.

> *Option*
> We will, however, retain your details on file and will contact you should a suitable position arise in the near future.

We would like to thank you for the interest shown in our company and wish you all the best for the future.

Yours sincerely,

_____

Name
Title

Appendix 4

SAMPLE LETTER REQUESTING REFERENCE

Confidential

Dear

Name of Candidate

The above-named is being considered for the position of _____ with this organisation and has given permission for us to contact you as a referee. I should be grateful if you would let me have the answers to the following questions. Your response will, of course, be treated as strictly confidential.

- In what capacity was the candidate employed?
- How long was the candidate employed by your organisation?
- How many days was the candidate absent during the period of employment?
- What was his/her reason for leaving?
- What was his/her salary, or rate of pay, on leaving your organisation?
- Would you re-employ?

Thank you for your assistance in this matter. A stamped addressed envelope is enclosed for your convenience.

Yours sincerely,

_____

Name
Title

SAMPLE APPRAISAL FORM

XXX Company

PERFORMANCE APPRAISAL FROM

Employee Name _____

Department _____

Date Commenced Employment_____

Appraisal Period_____

Manager's Name_____

Manager's Comments

How well has employee performed in relation to agreed objectives?

Employee's Strengths and Weaknesses

Future Plans and Actions (Training and Development)

Potential

Signed _____   **Date**_____

Employee's own comments on above assessment

_____
_____

Signed _____   **Date**_____

REFERENCES

Adams, J.S. (1963) "Towards an Understanding of Inequity" *Journal of Abnormal and Social Psychology*, November, pp. 422–36.

Alderfer, C.P. (1972) *Existence, Relatedness and Growth*, New York: Free Press.

Armstrong, M. (1993) *A Handbook of Personnel Management Practice*, London: Kogan Page.

Armstrong, M. (1999) *A Handbook of Human Resource Management Practice*, 7th edn, London: Kogan Page.

Armstrong, M. (2001) *A Handbook of Human Resource Management Practice*, 8th edn, London: Kogan Page.

Beardwell, I. and Holden, L. (1997) *Human Resource Management: A Contemporary Perspective*, London: Pitman.

Benge, E. (1944) *Job Evaluation and Merit Rating*, Washington: US National Foreman's Institute. Cited in Gunnigle, P., Heraty, N. and Morley, M. (1997) *Personnel and Human Resource Management: Theory and Practice in Ireland*, Dublin: Gill and Macmillan.

Carnall, C.A. (1990) *Managing Change in Organisations*, Hemel Hempstead: Prentice Hall.

Davies, R. (2001) "How to Boost Staff Retention" *People Management*, Vol. 7, No. 7.

Fennel, C. and Lynch, I. (1993) *Labour Law in Ireland*, Dublin: Gill and Macmillan.

Fisher, C.D., Schoenfeldt, L.F. and Shaw, J.B. (1998) *Human Resource Management*, 4th edn, Boston: Houghton Mifflin.

Foot, M. and Hook, C. (2002) *Introducing Human Resource Management*, 3rd edn, Harlow: Financial Times Prentice Hall.

Gibb, S. and Megginson, D. (1993) "Inside Corporate Mentoring Schemes: A New Agenda of Concerns" *Personnel Review*, Vol. 22, No. 1, pp. 40–54. Cited in Torrington, D. and Hall, L. (1998) *Human Resource Management*, 4th edn, London: Prentice Hall.

Graham, H.T. and Bennett, R. (1998) *Human Resources Management*, London: Pitman Publishing.

Guest, D. (1987) "Human Resource Management and Industrial Relations" *Journal of Management Studies*, Vol. 24, No. 5, pp. 503–21.

Gunnigle, P. and Flood, P. (1990) *Personnel Management in Ireland*, Dublin: Gill and Macmillan.

Gunnigle, P., Heraty, N. and Morley, M. (1997) *Personnel and Human Resource Management: Theory and Practice in Ireland*, Dublin: Gill and Macmillan.

Heery, E. and Noon, M. (2001) *A Dictionary of Human Resource Management*, Great Britain: Oxford University Press.

Herzberg, F. (1966) *Work and the Nature of Man*, Cleveland: World.

Hill, J. and Trist, E. (1955) "Changes in Accidents and other Absences with Length of Service" *Human Relations*, 8 May 1955. Cited in Gunnigle, P., Heraty, N. and Morley, M. (1997) *Personnel and Human Resource Management: Theory and Practice in Ireland*, Dublin: Gill and Macmillan.

Kahn-Freund, O. (1977) *Labour and the Law*, London: Stevens. Cited in Gunnigle, P., McMahon G. and Fitzgerald, G. (1995) *Industrial Relations in Ireland: Theory and Practice*, Dublin: Gill and Macmillan.

Kirkpatrick, D.L. (1959, 1960) "Techniques for Evaluating Training Programs" *Journal of the American Society of Training Directors*, Vol. 13, Nos 3–9, pp. 21–6; Vol. 14, Nos 13–18, pp. 28–32. Cited in Goldstein, I.L. (1993) *Training in Organisations*, California: Brooks/Cole.

Kotter, J.P. and Schlesinger, L.A. (1979) "Choosing Strategies for Change" *Harvard Business Review*, Vol. 57, No. 2, p. 106.

Latham, G.P. and Wexley, K.N. (1981) *Increasing Productivity through Performance Appraisal*, Wokingham: Addison-Wesley. Cited in Torrington, D. and Hall, L. (1998) *Human Resource Management*, 4th edn, London: Prentice Hall.

Lawler, E. (1977) "Reward Systems" in J. Hackman and J. Suttle (eds) *Improving Life at Work: Behavioural Science Approaches to Organisational Change*, New York: Goodyear.

McClelland, D. (1961) *The Achieving Society*, Princeton, New Jersey: Van Nostrand.

McGregor, D. (1960) *The Human Side of Enterprise*, New York: McGraw-Hill.

Maslow, A.H. (1943) "A Theory of Human Motivation" *Psychological Review*, Vol. 50, July, pp. 370–96.

Muchinsky, P. (1986) "Personnel Selection Methods" in C. Cooper and I. Robertson (eds) *International Review of Industrial and Organizational Psychology*, New York: Wiley.

Pettinger, R. (1994) *Introduction to Management*, London: Macmillan.

Reilly, R. and Chao, G. (1982) "Validity and Fairness of Some Alternative Employee Selection Procedures" *Personnel Psychology*, Vol. 35, No. 1–62. Cited in Muchinsky, P. (1986) "Personnel Selection Methods" in C. Cooper and I. Robertson (eds) *International Review of Industrial and Organizational Psychology*, New York: Wiley.

Roberts, G. (1997) *Recruitment and Selection: A Competency Approach*, Institute of Personnel and Development, London. Cited in Armstrong, M. (1999) *A Handbook of Human Resource Management Practice*, 7th edn, London: Kogan Page.

Rogers, C.R. (1947) "Some Observations on the Organisation of Personality" *American Psychologist*, Vol. 2, pp. 358–68.

Scott, J.F. (2000) *English and Communications for Business Students*, 4th edn, Dublin: Gill and Macmillan.

Woolcott, L.A. and Unwin, W.R. (1983) *Mastering Business Communication*, London: Macmillan.

INDEX